Discourse, Identity, and China's Internal Migration

ENCOUNTERS
Series Editors: Professor Jan Blommaert, *Tilburg University, The Netherlands*, Professor Ben Rampton, *Kings College London, UK,* Jens Normann Jørgensen, *University of Copenhagen, Denmark,* Anna De Fina, *Georgetown University, USA* and Marco Jacquemet, *University of San Francisco*

The Encounters series sets out to explore diversity in language from a theoretical and an applied perspective. So the focus is both on the linguistic encounters, inequalities and struggles that characterise post-modern societies and on the development, within sociocultural linguistics, of theoretical instruments to explain them. The series welcomes work dealing with such topics as heterogeneity, mixing, creolization, bricolage, cross-over phenomena, polylingual and polycultural practices. Another high-priority area of study is the investigation of processes through which linguistic resources are negotiated, appropriated and controlled, and the mechanisms leading to the creation and maintenance of sociocultural differences. The series welcomes ethnographically oriented work in which contexts of communication are investigated rather than assumed, as well as research that shows a clear commitment to close analysis of local meaning making processes and the semiotic organisation of texts.

Full details of all the books in this series and of all our other publications can be found on http://www.multilingual-matters.com, or by writing to Multilingual Matters, St Nicholas House, 31–34 High Street, Bristol BS1 2AW, UK.

ENCOUNTERS
Series Editors: Jan Blommaert, *Tilburg University, The Netherlands,* Ben Rampton, *Kings College London, UK,* Jens Normann Jørgensen, *University of Copenhagen, Denmark,* Anna De Fina, *Georgetown University, USA* and Marco Jacquemet, *University of San Francisco*

Discourse, Identity, and China's Internal Migration
The Long March to the City

Dong Jie

MULTILINGUAL MATTERS
Bristol • Buffalo • Toronto

Library of Congress Cataloging in Publication Data
A catalog record for this book is available from the Library of Congress.
Discourse, Identity, and China's Internal Migration: The Long March to the City/
Dong Jie.
Encounters: 1
Includes bibliographical references and index.
1. Chinese language--Discourse analysis. 2. Sociolinguistics--China. 3. China--
Emigration and immigration--Social aspects. 4. Children of migrant laborers--China.
I. Jie, Dong, 1975-
P302.15.C4D57 2011
306.440951--dc22 2011015602

British Library Cataloguing in Publication Data
A catalogue entry for this book is available from the British Library.

ISBN-13: 978-1-84769-420-1 (hbk)
ISBN-13: 978-1-84769-419-5 (pbk)

Multilingual Matters
UK: St Nicholas House, 31–34 High Street, Bristol, BS1 2AW, UK.
USA: UTP, 2250 Military Road, Tonawanda, NY 14150, USA.
Canada: UTP, 5201 Dufferin Street, North York, Ontario, M3H 5T8, Canada.

Copyright © 2011 Dong Jie.

All rights reserved. No part of this work may be reproduced in any form or by any means without permission in writing from the publisher.

Typeset by Techset Composition Ltd., Salisbury, UK.
Printed and bound in Great Britain by Short Run Press Ltd.

*For my mother Wang Shulan
and my father Dong Wenchao*

Contents

Acknowledgements ix
Transcription Symbols and Conventions xi

1   Introduction: The Long March to the City: An Ethnography
    of Discourse and Layered Identities among China's
    Internal Migrants.. 1
    Identities and Coca-Cola Cans 1
    Identity and Identity Studies................................ 4
    An Alternative Approach.................................... 10
    Overview of the Book 16
    Summary.. 21

2   A Roadmap into the Issue 23
    Introduction 23
    Social and Sociolinguistic Backgrounds..................... 24
    Fieldwork Issues 36
    Summary.. 42

3   Scale 1: Interaction... 45
    Introduction 45
    Central Concepts: Space, Scale and Monoglot Ideology 45
    Space, Accent and Identity Construction.................... 53
    Navigating accents and space 58
    Summary.. 65

4   Scale 2: Metapragmatic Discourses............................. 68
    Introduction 68
    Central Concepts: Speech Community and Ethnolinguistic
        Identity 68
    Language Ideology, Speech Community and Identity.......... 70
    Summary.. 84

5	Scale 3: Institutions	87
	Introduction	87
	Central Concepts: Abnormality, Stigma and Modernity	88
	Abnormal Identities	91
	Summary	110
6	Conclusions and Reflections	113
	Back to the Coca-Cola Can	113
	Theoretical Reflections	117
	Empirical Reflections	127
	Methodological Reflections	134

Appendix 1: Overview of Data Collection 138

Appendix 2: Chinese Texts and Pinyin Transcripts of Examples 140

References 146

Index 155

Acknowledgements

This book has grown out of a deep curiosity about migrant workers and their children in Beijing, who play an important role in the rapidly changing society and yet who remain invisible in many ways. My initial thoughts and observations of the migrant community gradually took shape through long discussions with Jan Blommaert, a wonderful colleague and friend. I would like to thank him for supporting me all the way through this project with tremendous sympathy and encouragement. I want to thank Sjaak Kroon for the enormous amount of time he invested in me and in my research, for his trust and confidence and for him being a constant source of inspiration. I also am indebted to Normann Jørgensen who read through the final draft; without his careful readings and critical comments this book would have never reached its present form.

During my stay at the Department of Language and Culture Studies, Tilburg University, I was always positioned in a comfortable academic environment, provided with magnificent facilities for research, and surrounded by friendly colleagues who were always ready to discuss my research and to help with all other issues in life. Kasper Juffermans – my office-mate – was a great example with whom I had many intellectually challenging and enjoyable discussions. In the various stages of this research project, Gao Yihong, Adrian Blackledge, Li Wei, Hans Siebers, Catherine Walter, Ben Rampton, Ad Backus, Han Jialing, Caroline McGlynn, Peter Martin (whom we sadly lost recently), Jeanne Kurvers, Massimiliano Spotti and the people of the NORFACE seminars in 2007 and 2008, among many others whom I found impossible to list in this limited space, gave me valuable advice and supported me in different ways, to whom I wish to express my sincere gratitude. Moreover, the pupils and teachers at the two schools where I did my fieldwork deserve my greatest respect and thanks for their trust, their friendliness and their willingness to be brilliant informants. A special word of thanks should go to Carine

Zebedee, the superb departmental secretary who saw my work through the final editing process.

This book is dedicated to my parents, for their unconditional love – 爸妈, 我希望你们为我感到骄傲. I am immensely grateful to my parents whose help with childcare made this book possible. Finally, my son Li Enjia, now 30 months, has been a wonderful witness of this book, and my thanks to him for letting me concentrate on this book while waiting for my company.

Dong Jie
Beijing
16 February 2011

Transcription Symbols and Conventions

_	(Underline) stress
=	Interruption or next utterance following immediately
[ ]	IPA phonetic transcription
{ }	Transcriber's comment
* *	Segment quieter than surrounding talk, or weaker than the rest of the sentence
( )	Omitted part in the utterance
Bold	Marks the shifts among the accents

Unless otherwise specified, the translations from Chinese are my own.

Unless otherwise specified, the contents between brackets are my own additions or comments.

Chapter 1
Introduction: The Long March to the City: An Ethnography of Discourse and Layered Identities among China's Internal Migrants

Identities and Coca-Cola Cans

'Identity' is the focus of this research. Identity-making discourses such as 'he is a Dutchman' and 'she is a teacher' frequently circulate in our daily lives. In conferences we wear a badge with our names so that our interlocutors have an idea of whom they are talking to; while travelling abroad, people should remember to carry their ID, that is, passports or identification cards, and be prepared for potential police inspection – this can be crucial for groups such as Turks and Africans in some of the Western European metropolises; on meeting new colleagues we often exchange information on where we come from, our nationalities, what jobs did we do before. And as a Chinese, I find myself engaged in a constant task of explaining my name: which is my given name, which is my surname and in what circumstances I would rather use an English name.

Indeed, we are involved in identity rituals around every corner of our life. The question it raises – the question of 'who am I' – often touches something dearest to our hearts, something we hold fast, whereas a challenge of it by others can easily offend us. Identity means different things on different occasions – 'who I am' depends on whom I am talking to, in what circumstances and from what perspectives. Let me illustrate this point with a metaphor (see Figure 1.1a, b and c).

Figure 1.1a gives a front view of a Coca-Cola can[1] and shows some of its defining features: its cylinder shape, its easily recognisable logo, trademark and so forth. It can be seen as a 'normal' view of a Coca-Cola can – a view that fits in with the stereotype we usually have. However, if we look

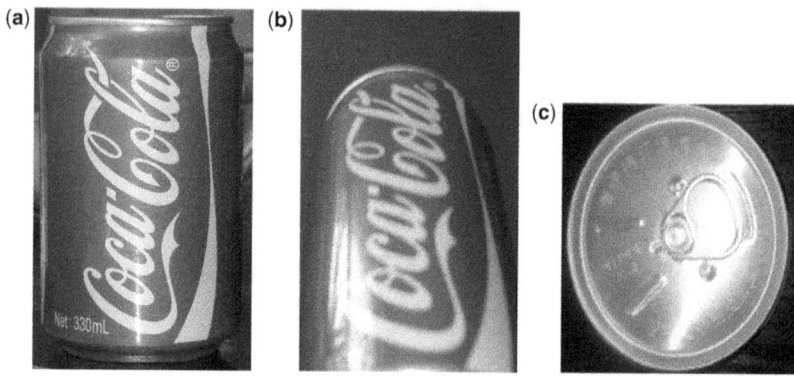

Figure 1.1 (a) Front view, (b) bottom-side view and (c) vertical view of a Coca-Cola can

at the can again from a lower angle (Figure 1.1b), we get a rather different picture: its cylinder shape is distorted, some features are exaggerated, such as the initial 'C' of the logo, while other features fall out of sight. An even more unusual picture is the one shown in Figure 1.1c – the same can be observed from the top. At this level, the distinguishing details of a Coca-Cola can (the logo, the design, etc.) are replaced by a set of more abstract features – metal, with an opening ring, and a sentence urging the consumer to recycle the can. It could be a Pepsi can or a beer can. Observing the can from this angle, one could not tell whether the rest of the can – its cylinder-shaped body – exists or not.

Each time it is the can; the can is all of that. It is still the same can, but we end up with different descriptions observing it from different positions; the positions are vertically ordered: observed from a lower angle (Figure 1.1b), some details of the can are distorted, exaggerated or neglected whereas enough features remain for us to tell what it is. Our gaze then is moved upwards and we obtain a 'normal' stereotypical view (Figure 1.1a) that fits in with our expected image of a Coca-Cola can. On a higher scale when we look down from the top (Figure 1.1c), the defining details disappear, and what we see are some abstract and rigid features of any metal can. Each observation is partially similar and partially different and none of it shows a picture of the whole can – every description is conditioned by the position from which we observe it. There are an infinite number of scale levels that we may consider observing. I have taken three scales to demonstrate that one scale is not enough and a full analysis involves taking into account various scales. I could focus on more scales, but chose three so that we could more clearly see that a social phenomenon at one scale is different at another scale.

The examination of identity construction is of little difference from observing a Coca-Cola can. Focusing solely on lower level observation – the level of local interaction – we may obtain detailed yet distorted understandings of identity. Analysing only the 'normal' view – the level of people's discursive evaluation on their own and others' identities – we risk overlooking the 'not-so-normal' views of identity making. Positioning ourselves at the top level – the level of administrative realities – identity categorisation becomes rigid and abstract. None of the current paradigms in identity studies from a single level – whatever level that is – is sufficient, because social phenomena such as identity making are never singular and homogeneous, but are always layered and multifaceted, and all aspects have to be described and analysed comprehensively. What we need is a more sophisticated approach that revolves around an image of social reality as structured into different scales, which attends to the rules and conventions that operate at the different scale levels, and which uncovers the interplay and collaboration of different scales in one situated event.

There are compelling reasons to develop such an approach, and perhaps the most compelling one is the ever-increasing complexity of discursive processes of identity construction in the context of rapid linguistic and cultural exchanges among various communities as a result of transnational as well as intra-national migrations – what we usually call 'globalisation'. The empirical data of this book have been collected in China, where intense rural–urban migration has been going on since the early 1980s. The rural–urban migration, also known as 'internal' migration, results in complicated sociolinguistic environments in which regional accents and dialects become salient markers of identity, projecting prestige and opportunity, or stigma and social inequality. The phenomenal rural–urban migration in China offers an enormously rich research potential in the discursive processes of identity construction; yet, there has been limited research focused on this field so far (but see Dong, 2009; Dong & Blommaert, 2009).

This book is therefore a contribution to filling this gap through a close look at the discursive processes of identity construction among Chinese internal migrants. There are two objectives in the present study. First, I propose and argue for a three-scale theoretical framework, a scalar structure that organises various levels and facets of identity making practice in the context of migration and globalisation. It is a selection of discursive scales indeed, but a salient selection of which all three scale-levels articulate different types of identity building discourses. We see more elaboration on this point in section 'An Alternative Approach'. My broader purpose, related to the first one, is to draw attention to a series of social processes through which we are able to gain an insight into transitions in Chinese society and the (re-)formation of social structure. The mass internal migration that forms the backdrop of this study, for instance, reactivates diacritics of social class stratification in a society that used to ideologically describe itself as egalitarian. Although the specific objects of such social processes considered in this book are sociolinguistic forms, these forms – the discursive practice of migrant identity construction – are arguably part of, and serve as a reflection of, the processual and dynamic social transition and reformation.

This introductory chapter opens with a metaphor of the general theoretical framework that I construct throughout the book. In what follows, I provide a brief account of several basic assumptions that underpin the arguments of this book, and further answer the question concerning why the field of identity study needs such a new approach focusing on the scalar nature of social reality. In section 'An Alternative Approach', I elaborate on the proposed approach and explain how it has emerged from fieldwork and how it is theorised. I then outline the book in the section 'Overview of the Book', and sum up the study by reflecting on what I achieve in this chapter in the last section.

Identity and Identity Studies

'Identity' has been a popular research topic in various social-scientific disciplines ranging from psychology, sociology, anthropology and history, to linguistics, literature, education and others. Many kinds of identities have been studied, for example, ethnicity, race, class, gender identity, national identity, learning identity and so on (e.g. Block, 2006; Butler, 1990; Cameron, 1992; De Fina *et al.*, 2006; Gao, 2009; Gao & Xiu, 2004; Gao *et al.*, 2007a, 2007b; Hewitt, 1986; Kulick, 1998; Norton-Pierce, 2000; Rampton, 1999; Spotti, 2007; Willis, 1981; Wodak, 1997; Wortham, 2006, to name just a few). It is not my intention to give a comprehensive account of identity studies, and such a job is indeed impossible for the limited space of this book. Rather, I begin with a few assumptions and understandings of identity construction that are fundamental to this particular study, and then briefly evaluate two defining trends of recent discursive studies on identity construction. These evaluations will demonstrate the need for an alternative approach.

The first point I want to stress is that identity is not something one possesses, but it is constructed in social practice. This runs against the essentialist notion of the 'self' as given, core, natural and essentially innate to the person (Bucholtz *et al.*, 1999; Potter, 2003). Identities are eminently social and performative in nature, being negotiated, enacted, constructed and perceived in social practices; indeed, we have seen various studies demonstrating that identity is a dynamic, flexible and changeable project (Foucault, 1984), such as research in gender identity (Butler, 1990), in ethnicity (Roosens, 1989) and national identity (Hobsbawm & Ranger, 1983).

Second, I do not see 'identity' as an individual, monolithic construct, but as a repertoire of identities, which suggests that people perform highly complex and ambiguous identities, shifting between as well as displaying simultaneously their multiple identities in social interactions. Moreover, people construct identities out of particular identity building resources (Blommaert, 2005a: 203). As access to such resources is often unequally distributed, identities that are built through identity building resources are layered and stratified. For instance, acquiring a prestige accent can be costly, if we think of how much people would invest in learning English with a standard American or BBC accent across the world, and there are people who never have the capacity to enact a highly ranked identity due to the lack of access to the highly ranked accent as an identity building resource.

Third, identities are achieved as well as ascribed, and consequently, identity processes are negotiation processes. Achieved identity, also known as subscribed identity or inhabited identity, refers to a 'self-constructed and self-performed identity ... through which people claim allegiance to a group' (Blommaert, 2005a: 253). In contrast to achieved identity, ascribed identity is an 'identity attributed to someone by others ... including that someone in a socially defined category' (Blommaert, 2005a: 251). In this sense, an identity has to be negotiated and recognised by others in order to be established in and as social reality, and more often than not identities are imposed by others rather than claimed by oneself. Examples can be found in othering processes, of which the use of pronouns such as 'we', 'us', 'they', 'them' often signals shifts of alignments to different social groups (see also Goffman, 1981).[2]

Having outlined several basic understandings of identity construction, I evaluate two major approaches of recent identity studies – Conversational Analysis (CA) and Critical Discourse Analysis (CDA). Both approaches share the basic understandings about identity construction laid out above, but are deeply divided over theoretical and methodological issues – notably over the perceptions of the relationship between discourse and society. It is not a novel task to contrast CA and CDA (see e.g. Blommaert, 2005a; De Fina *et al.*, 2006), and the division between the two approaches is not confined to identity studies (Chouliaraki & Fairclough, 1999; Fairclough, 1996; Schegloff, 1999; Widdowson, 1995, 1996, 1998). The contrast between them, however, is particularly remarkable in identity studies, as the discursive processes of identity construction are precisely about the relationship between discourse and society. Following the evaluations of these two approaches, I will argue that, although important and influential, neither CA nor CDA is sufficient for an adequate study of the discursive processes of identity construction, and I will propose an alternative approach that is able to address such complex and critical issues.

Let us first take a look at CA. In terms of conception of the relationship between discourse and society, research within this tradition typically emphasises interactional events between immediate participants within the immediate local context. Schegloff claims that an interactional event has to be analysed

> in its endogenous constitution, what it was for the parties involved in it, in its course, as embodied and displayed in the very details of its realization – can we even begin to explore what forms a critical approach to it might take, and what political issue, if any, it allows us to address. (Schegloff, 1997: 168)

In terms of methodology, CA refrains from using 'a political or cultural frame of analysis' (Antaki & Widdicombe, 1998: 5); instead, it advocates the use of 'internal analysis' – a technical analysis internal to the interactional event at hand, that 'talk-in-interaction does provide ... an Archimedean point ... internal to the object of analysis itself' (Schegloff, 1997: 184). In the domain of identity studies, CA sees identity categories to be exclusively performed, practised and enacted by the participants engaged in the interactional events. Identities are therefore products of the interactional events at hand and the only relevant context is the immediate local context, although identity is one of the few topics on which 'non-local' context is sometimes allowed to play a role (e.g. D'hondt, 2001; Li Wei, 1998; Rampton, 1995; Zhu, 2008). In general, with several exceptions outlined below, CA stresses 'talk-in-interaction', and this conceptual position has a methodological consequence – that texts are often analysed internally, and researchers are discouraged from looking at issues on the macro levels of social reality. As a consequence, what we often see in CA research is the replication of interactions at hand and negotiation of identities at the level of individual interactional events.

A remarkable exception within CA can be found in Rampton's research on sociolinguistic styles and styling practice through everyday interactions in multilingual schools in inner London, which combines CA with broadly drawn social theories, in an attempt to avoid a reductive analysis of linguistic processes (cf. Rampton, 1995, 1999, 2006). Another exception is D'hondt's integration of membership categorisation into his research on quarrels among Dar es Salaam adolescents, which offers firm connections between conversational work and observations of social structure (D'hondt, 2001). In both instances, we see that the authors, despite strong allegiances to a CA framework, allow wider aspects of context – non-situational context – to be drawn into the analysis, and allow such broader contexts to become critically relevant to the analysis.

As for identity studies, seeing identity as performed and enacted is a well-established understanding, and it has been addressed as a first basic assumption of this book. It will be problematic, however, to claim that identities only emerge out of interactional events and are only to be analysed internally. Examples can be found in the street corner data of Chapter 3, in which I, the fieldworker, encounter a street vendor who runs a small business of selling steamed dumplings as breakfast food. The conversations between the street vendor and me indeed articulate a clear process of identity negotiation. However, even before any interpersonal conversation occurs, both participants are likely to associate stereotypical identity categories with each other, that is, working class vs. middle class, migrant vs. local. Such categories have been pre-inscribed in and circulated through public, institutional and media discourses. That is to say, the identity categories of migrant worker and urban middle class have been moved into place at a higher level long before the interactional event, and they condition the negotiation process at lower levels of communicative exchanges. And while at the level of everyday interaction no one can be said to 'have' identities – there is always a negotiation process involved – at this higher level of social structure we can indeed say that we 'have' identities. There are limits to the negotiation process. The example above challenges both the conceptual position of 'talk-in-interaction' and the methodological hegemony of 'internal analysis', as we observe that local interactional events are constrained by identity processes at higher levels, that participants engaged in a linguistic exchange are not free to construct and claim *any* identity and that factors 'out of interaction' have to be taken into account when researching identities in interaction. The interactional construction of identities, in sum, is *constrained*, it is not a process of infinite indeterminacy, but rather develops within a determined space. This, I should note, is not an essentialist position. It is an empirically realistic one, and it accounts for the simple observation that I, as an adult, cannot speak *as* a child. I can speak *like* a child, and I can imitate a child. But no matter how hard I try, I can never *be* a child again.

Let us now turn to CDA. In contrast to CA's stance on the relationship between discourse and society, CDA maintains that discourse is socially shaped and socially shaping:

> it is an important characteristic of the economic, social and cultural changes of late modernity that they exist as discourses... and that the processes that are taking place outside discourse are substantively shaped by these discourses. (Chouliaraki & Fairclough, 1999: 4)

The distinctiveness of CDA, argues Wodak (1997: 173), lies in the relationships between language and society, and between analysis and the practices analysed. Such relationships include the 'opaque as well as transparent structural relationships of dominance, discrimination, power and control as manifested in language' (Wodak, 1995: 204).

Along this line of argument, identity studies often (although not always, see e.g. Blackledge, 2005; Fairclough, 1992) prioritise the political and ideological dimensions in the formation of identities, and see identities as being socially formed, conditioned and imposed by political and ideological contexts, particularly by power relations at institutional levels. Examples can be found in Wodak's study of doctor–patient discourse (Wodak, 1997), in which the dominance of 'white male doctors' is unquestionably introduced as the factual context of the discourse data, and the predefined doctor–patient power relations are imposed onto, and (more often than not), confirmed by the discourse analysis. Unsurprisingly, what we often see in CDA research is not unveiling hidden power relations but confirming the researcher's contextualising narratives given before the data analysis (Blommaert, 2005a; Briggs, 1997; Schegloff, 1997).

As a fieldworker, however, I often observe identity building moments that are contradictory to my expectations, expectations that are derived from an awareness of the wider social and political contexts. As we see in Chapters 3, 4 and 5, the primary school case highlights migrant identity construction in a publicly funded school that is populated by both local Beijing and migrant pupils. I entered the fieldwork site with a package of assumptions about what would happen in such a school; for example, the difficulties that migrant pupils would have in getting access to public schools in urban areas, the potential tension between local and migrant pupils, and the possible discriminations against migrant pupils from local teachers and so forth. Most of these assumptions came from public and media discourses. However, I encountered overwhelming evidence at the interpersonal level that local and migrant pupils made friends with each other, that migrant pupils identified themselves as local, and that local teachers invested enormous amounts of extra time and attention in their migrant pupils. It was only when my gaze moved to the level of teacher's evaluative remarks on pupil performance that the differentiation between local and migrant pupils started to emerge, and the political and ideological context became a visible dimension of migrant identity making. We will look at the emergence and definition of the three scales in the next section. The fieldwork evidence questions CDA's claims that power relations, political context and ideology determine how identities are formulated and perceived at the ground level of linguistic and communicative exchanges. CDA functions well in a particular dimension – a political and ideological dimension – but there appears to be a far larger room of identity negotiation at various levels and dimensions, and a great deal of deviation from assumed identity patterns, particularly if we look at the identity construction among school pupils (cf. also Spotti, 2007; Wortham, 2006). So just as we see in our critique of CA, here too we need to move to a more nuanced position. The processes of power that CDA focuses on occur *at certain scale levels*. At other scale levels, we see entirely different processes at work.

To summarise, we briefly evaluate two important but deeply divided approaches of identity studies – Conversation Analysis and Critical Discourse Analysis. The two approaches are polarised on several theoretical and methodological issues. The differences are mainly derived from the different perceptions on the relations between language and society. In the field of identity studies, CA's 'talk-in-interaction' stance and 'internal analysis' analytical method is in sharp contrast to CDA's emphasis on the imposition of power relations, institutional, political and ideological contexts onto identities.

Both positions, however, do not withstand empirical control. None of them offers a comprehensive account of the *whole* of the social process that yields identities, because such a process develops on different scales. It is, in other words, not one united process, but a compound process that has several levels. The process, as I said earlier, confronts us with the problem of the Coca-Cola can. Observation at the interpersonal level (the first scale of the three-scale framework), a level on which everyday communicative events occur, often show that egalitarian ideas are circulated among teachers and pupils, that migrant pupils function well and that they achieve, to some extent, an urban identity through interactions with local teachers and pupils. As soon as my attention moves upwards to the metapragmatic level (the second scale), a level on which people articulate comments and evaluations on language and identity, the migrant pupils' newly achieved identity claims are often disqualified by the comments and evaluations of their urban counterparts and local teachers. Moving further upwards to the institutional level (the third scale), a level on which discourses are circulated in the public and institutional sphere, one finds more rigid identity categorisations – migrant workers' rural identity is indisputably marked in their *hukou*, an official household registration that groups people into rural or urban populations, and migrant children are officially rural residents if their parents are under such a category – it is irrelevant as to whether the children were born in the host city or not and whether they identify themselves as urban children or not. These fieldwork observations and reflections lead to the agenda I propose in this book, that the discursive process of identity making ought to be studied at different scale levels, that identities of one level interact with those of another, and that identities negotiated and constructed at one level may well be denied at another level. I have referred to this framework and used the can metaphor as an introduction. In the next section, I will describe it in detail as an alternative approach to what we have commonly used so far.

An Alternative Approach

Recall the Coca-Cola can metaphor given at the beginning of this chapter: observed from a lower level (Figure 1.1b) some details of the can are distorted, exaggerated or neglected whereas enough features remain for us to tell what it is; moving up the scale, we get a 'normal' view (Figure 1.1a) that fits in with our stereotype of a Coca-Cola can; on a higher scale (Figure 1.1c), the defining details are replaced by abstract and rigid features of any metal can – each time it is the same can, but observing it from different positions results in different accounts of description which are partly different and partly similar. No single description is complete because each description is defined by the specific position we take to observe. In terms of understanding identities, I do not attempt to offer a complete analytic model; rather, my aim is to identify and examine different positions we can take to analyse identity construction in, and as, a stratified social reality. This is to avoid essentialism in the study of identity, as identity is not one essential item that one possesses, but a layered and multidimensional process that is enacted and performed in social practice. The alternative approach to identity construction proposed here revolves around a scalar image of social reality, a social reality that is structured into different scales. Each scale is characterised by norms and conventions of its own, which allow certain things to happen, and prevent other things from being played out. A more comprehensive analysis of social phenomena demands an investigation of the various scales and their features. If we fail to attend to them we are trapped in a unidimensional and reductionist view of social reality that assumes homogeneity and uniformity, and assumes a single set of rules and conventions governing the different scales and the features of these scales. Before moving on, I shall briefly introduce and explain two notions that are central to the three-scale framework and will appear in every analytical chapter of this book: indexicality and scale.

Indexicality is the link between linguistic signs and social meanings. Apart from referential or denotational meaning, an utterance also *points to* social meaning that is interpretive within the particular social occasion in which it is produced. An utterance often *indexes* stereotypically associated features of the speaker (gender, ethnicity, age, social class, etc.), of the relationship between the speaker and the hearer (employer and employee, parent and child, customer and shopkeeper, doctor and patient and so on), and of the social context in which it is produced (cf. Agha, 2007; Blommaert, 2005a; Johnstone *et al.*, 2006; Silverstein, 1996, 2003). The notion of indexicality allows us to analyse a communicative act beyond its linguistic dimension to its contextual and social dimension. For the arguments in this book, indexicality is the connection that links linguistic, metapragmatic and institutional scales of identity construction.

Scale is a spatiotemporal metaphor that has been used in social theories such as history and social geography (cf. Swyngedouw, 1996; Uitermark, 2002). It is also a key concept in Wallerstein's World-Systems Analysis, which describes the world as a system of structurally unequal parts organised on a continuum of layered scales (Wallerstein, 1983, 2000, 2001). In the domain of sociolinguistics, the notion of scale is used to address sociolinguistic phenomena in globalised social reality, in an attempt to understand society through the study of language (Blommaert, 2005a, 2006a; Blommaert *et al.*, 2005a, 2005b). For the analysis of identity construction in this book, 'scale' provides an image of society and of social phenomena that are not unified and homogeneous, but are stratified and polycentric. Chapter 3 elaborates further on this notion. So far I have used 'layer' and 'level', and I will also use 'scale' as the core element of the vertical and layered structure of identity construction.

The notions of 'indexicality' and 'scale' work together to build the scalar framework I argue for in this study, in the way that 'scale' functions as the skeleton of the framework, and 'indexicality' connects one scale to another. Out of a magnitude of possible scales, I select three specific ones, that is, the linguistic and communicative exchange scale, the metapragmatic scale and the public and institutional scale. I select these three scales because each of them has had a more or less separate life in the literature on identity. The communicative exchange scale has been central to the concerns of CA; the metapragmatic scale is the target of a lot of social-psychological work on identity (e.g. Potter & Wetherell, 1987); and the public and institutional scale is central to much work in CDA. Combining these scales in one analysis may draw in the strengths of each of these approaches, while also avoiding their shortcomings. The three scales are a selection of various social dimensions, but it is a salient selection in that the three scales focus on different identity discourses. There can be numerous scales, and these three scales are selected to demonstrate that any one scale is inadequate in researching social phenomena that are always multifaceted and polycentric. In what follows, I show that the three scales are connected in relevant ways.

Scale 1: Linguistic and communicative exchange scale

At the linguistic and communicative scale, trivial, everyday linguistic exchanges occur, which can be illustrated by the bottom-side view of the Coca-Cola can. Identities constructed at this scale often have the characteristics of being fluid, flexible and ever changing; small linguistic features index 'big' social issues such as one's place of origin, social class, race, ethnicity, gender, age, profession and so forth. At the linguistic and communicative scale people often claim, enact and shift between different identities and such identities are ratified, challenged or denied here-and-now. Identities constructed at this scale are to be distinguished from what are sometime addressed as 'small' identities as in Georgakopoulou (2006), or 'situational' identities (Zimmerman, 1998) in CA. Research attention in small or situational identities has been focused on and around the interlocutors' turn taking, code switching, choice of style and so on; in this research trend, identities are treated as intrinsic and endogenous to the local interactions between participants and are not 'transportable', as Zimmerman (1998) describes, across interactions and situations. Identities constructed at the linguistic and communicative exchange scale, however, are different from 'small' or 'situational' identities: although small and situational, lower-level scale identities often reflect and are conditioned by identities at higher-level scales. The street vendor in Chapter 3 adopts a local Beijing accent and claims an identity as such, and the claimed identity, or what we call 'inhabited identity', is taken on board by me as the other interlocutor in the interpersonal linguistic exchanges; however, if he, for instance, attempts to send his children to a public school in Beijing, the claimed identity will turn out to be of little use, and what matters will be his identity categorisation in official documents. Here we see that identities at the lower scale – the linguistic and communicative exchange scale – are fluid and flexible, but often interact with and are conditioned by identities at higher-level scales.

Scale 2: Metapragmatic discourse scale

The metapragmatic discourse scale is the scale of people's comments, evaluative remarks, discourses and reflections on their own as well as other people's linguistic features and language use. Identities constructed at this scale typically revolve around explicit evaluative framework that is informed by language ideology. Different from linguistic features and communicative styles that index identities on the linguistic and communicative exchange scale, metapragmatic discourses make identity making processes explicit in the way that people articulate identity comments and categorise themselves and others into social groups. Identities are achieved as well as ascribed. For an identity to be established, it has to be ratified by others. Some identities claimed at the linguistic and communicative exchange scale may well be denied at the scale of metapragmatic discourses, whereas other identities can be imposed upon people at this scale. In fact, metapragmatic discourses are often major tools for 'othering', that is, for the production of ascribed identities. Examples can be found in the interactions between identities on the metapragmatic discourse scale and identities on the other scales, that is, scale of linguistic and communicative exchanges and the scale of public and institutional discourses. A migrant child (Hong in the primary school case in Chapter 4), who was born and lives in Beijing all her life, has inhabited an identity of being a local Beijing child. Her claimed identity is taken on board by me, a local Beijing person and class observer, because of her notable Beijing accent. This identity is challenged by her Beijing peer students and denied by her teacher, who comments that

> They {Hong and other migrant pupils}, well, they, they have all grown up in Beijing, they think they are Beijing people, but actually they are not. They are grade 1 and have no idea who they are; they think they live in Beijing and so they are Beijing people but they are not. (Field recording, 2007-06-21-V044)

The teacher's evaluative remarks – a metapragmatic discourse – on Hong's identity deny Hong's self-claimed local Beijing identity and attribute a migrant identity to her instead. This example shows the interface of the first two scales – the linguistic and communicative exchange scale and the metapragmatic discourse scale. Next, let us look at the third scale – the institutional and public discourse scale.

Scale 3: Institutional and public discourse scale

While on scale 1, identities were constructed through talk (situated and topical interactions), and on scale 2, identities were constructed through evaluative discourses on one's own and other people's communicative behaviour, identities on scale 3 are constructed through general, unspecific, socio-political discourses. Scale 3 is also metapragmatic in many ways, but it invokes different identity criteria: general socio-cultural rules of conduct, social norms, laws and regulations. And while the first two scales produce specific and individualised identities, scale 3 produces generic, categorical identities. The ascribed identity that Hong's teacher articulated (i.e. 'they think they are Beijing people, but actually they are not') is based on Hong's *hukou* record: although Hong speaks like a local Beijing child and she claims a local identity, she is 'actually' not, according to official documents that specify that she is a rural child and her place of residence is not Beijing. Such a categorisation emerges from the institutional and public discourses at the third scale – the scale at which media reports, legal status, policy papers and other public discourses function to construct or constrain identities. Recall viewing the Coca-Cola can from the top: it is the same can yet its defining details are overlaid by a set of abstract and rigid features that strictly categorise it to be a can. In legal documents, one becomes a particular type of case (an asylum seeker, a residence permit holder, for instance), a dossier, an object of administration and such bureaucratic identifications have a real (and often a decisive) effect on what one can get in everyday life, such as whether one has the right to remain in the country, whether one can move around freely, and in the case of China's internal migrant pupils, where they are entitled to free or subsidised education and whether they have access to social welfare and protection in the host city that they claim to identify with.

Examples of identity constructing discourses on this scale also include media reports on 'too many immigrants' – as what we often hear in the Western European context – and on immigrants' difficulties in finding jobs in the host country or region, 'they are taking our jobs'. The media discourses convey and circulate specific messages about immigrant identities and associate immigrant identities with a package of social meanings, such as being outsiders to society, competing for jobs with the local people, bringing their families and hence more immigrants, being and becoming social problems that require the invention of new policy tools and solutions (Dong, 2010b). All these messages contribute to an institutional and public discourse scale of identity building that conditions identity construction at the lower-level scales.

Identity construction on the institutional and public discourse scale has to be differentiated from the determining role of power relations and dominant ideology in framing identities advocated by CDA. As discussed in the previous section, CDA emphasises that identities are formed or imposed by political and ideological contexts, and thus often prioritises the political and ideological dimensions in the formation of identities over local discursive practice. The institutional and public discourse scale I propose here, however, refers not to the contextual effects on identity construction, but to the identities expressed, negotiated and perceived through institutional, public and media discourses, in which more rigid categorisations often occur. Identities constructed on this scale interact with those constructed on the linguistic and communicative exchange scale and on the metapragmatic discourse scale: an identity achieved on the linguistic and communicative exchange scale may be denied when it travels upwards to the metapragmatic discourse scale and the institutional and public discourse scale; and rigid categorisations on the institutional and public discourse scale may become invisible on lower scales, although they often tacitly shape what occurs at the lower levels.

To sum up, the three-scale framework of identity construction comprises: (1) the linguistic and communicative exchange scale on which 'small' everyday linguistic features index 'big' social processes, and identities established on this scale can be fluid, flexible and ever changing: (2) the metapragmatic discourse scale on which we encounter explicit evaluative discourses grounded in language ideologies: and (3) the institutional and public discourse scale, on which more rigid identity categorisations occur.

Having built a three-scale framework, we must be conscious that the framework does not encourage a mechanistic approach. Rather, the three scales also function in one spatiotemporally bound event. When we observe a social phenomenon, we can only observe it in its synchronic form; what we have to bear in mind, however, is that the synchronic event is a product of the interplay between different scale levels, a situated event that hides the operation of the rules and conventions of various scales. A social phenomenon always has an observational level on which it appears as spatiotemporally bound, unique, and simple, and an analytical level on which it appears as layered and structured. This duality is the key argument of this book, and it motivates the methodological options I take.

Overview of the Book

In this section I first give a brief account of the social and linguistic backgrounds of the study, and a description of the methodology I have employed in collecting and analysing the data. Chapter 2 is devoted to the extended discussion on the research backgrounds and methodology. Later in this section, I survey the fieldwork cases that are deployed to illustrate the three-scale theoretical framework. The detailed presentation and analysis of the cases can be found in the three analytical chapters: Chapters 3, 4 and 5. Chapter 6 draws conclusions and offers theoretical, empirical, as well as methodological reflections on the research.

Social and linguistic backgrounds

Population movements within China's borders – or internal migration – are part of globalisation processes, as we shall see in detail in the next chapter. They resemble the cross-border labour migrations in Europe some decades ago, in the sense that people 'emigrate' from their places of origin for better life opportunities, carrying their cultural and linguistic belongings with them to 'immigrant' countries such as the United Kingdom, France and the Netherlands in Western Europe, and in the case of China's internal migrants, to the metropolitan cities such as Beijing, Shanghai, Guangzhou, Shenzhen, as well as the eastern coastal regions that are commercially and industrially developed compared to the vast western, inland and rural areas in China. In Western Europe, the speed of immigration flow, immigrants' prolonged stay and eventual permanent settlement, among other factors, attract much public and research attention in various fields such as social inequality, education, community studies (e.g. Butler & Robson, 2003; Oria *et al.*, 2007; Raveaud & van Zanten, 2007; Reay, 2004a, 2004b). Similarly, the influx of China's rural labourers into urban areas has become an increasingly popular topic in the public as well as academic domains (e.g. Fan, 2004, 2005; Han, 2001; Lu, 2005; Lu & Zhang, 2001; Woronov, 2004; Zhang *et al.*, 2003).

The rural–urban migration in China started in the wake of dramatic economic reform and social changes in the 1980s. Before the reform, population movement was tightly controlled through *hukou*. The system was gradually relaxed from the 1980s onwards in response to the increase of labourer demand from the rapid growth of manufacture and service sectors in cities (Ma, 1999). The migrant population, according to a sampling survey conducted by the China National Statistics Bureau, reached 147,350,000 in 2005.[3] In Beijing alone, it is estimated that the migrant population was 3,570,000 by 2005, which was some 20% of the total population of Beijing, and this figure is increasing by 40% per year.[4] Migrants used to be mainly young male farmers working in towns and cities for a few months during a year; more recent investigations indicate that a high proportion tend to relocate as family units and stay longer in cities than before. They often do low-skilled jobs as construction workers, waiters, cleaners, domestic workers, shoe mender and so forth, jobs that urban citizens tend to avoid. They, thus, almost invariably enter the lowest strata of the working class, in an urban area that now also hosts a sizeable middle class. In Chapter 5, we will see that class differences can be played out in public discourses about migrants. The huge migrant population and the extended period of urban experiences give rise to the 'super-diversity' (Blommaert, 2009c; Vertovec, 2006) of people from various communities of the state, carrying regional accents and dialects, and resulting in ever more complex linguistic and sociolinguistic environments.

Linguistic differences are a salient mark of ethnic and regional group membership and place of origin in China that hosts at least 56 officially recognised ethnic groups. Many ethnic groups have their own languages; 'Chinese' is an umbrella term for the language spoken by the majority Han Chinese, which comprises many varieties. Linguists often categorise them into seven major dialects, and although many of them may not be mutually intelligible, they are generally considered to be 'dialects' (or *'fangyan'*, literally 'regional speech') in China (Hu, 1995; Ramsey, 1987). In the actual practice of social life, people sometimes link language varieties with particular places, as the term *fangyan* itself refers, for example, *Dongbei dialect* (the dialect of the north-east regions), *Henan dialect* (the dialect of Henan province).

Partly due to the mutual unintelligibility among China's many languages and dialects, there has been always a need for a common language in the centralised state-systems that characterised China's history. Putonghua, literally 'common speech', is a standardised variety of Mandarin spoken in Beijing and its nearby regions[5] (Ramsey, 1987). People acquire Putonghua through formal education, as it is institutionally supported as the language of instruction in schools, as well as the official language in the state's other institutions (Dong, 2010a). Being a language used for public life, Putonghua is translocal and affords social and geographic mobility, whereas dialects are mostly local and for private occasions. It is reported that 53% of the Chinese people are able to communicate in Putonghua (*China Daily*, 26-12-2004). The identity construction of migrant pupils is studied against such wider social contexts of population movements, regional inequality and linguistic as well as cultural diversity. Recent studies in effect show that the mass migrations from rural to urban centres have led to a shift in the sociolinguistic profile of the large cities in China. Migration, according to these studies, clearly strengthens the position of Putonghua and puts pressure on local dialects and linguistic varieties (Lei, 2009; Tsou, 2009; Van den Berg, 2009; Xu, 2009; Yu, 2009).

Ethnography

This research draws upon my ethnographic fieldwork among migrant workers and their children in Beijing in 2006 and 2009. The ethnographic study of language finds its roots in anthropology, which offers a distinct ontology and epistemology and situates language deeply in social life. An ethnographic approach is what Hymes (1980) calls a 'descriptive theory': an approach that is theoretical because it provides description in specific, methodologically and epistemologically grounded ways. Although ethnography can be used in different theoretical frameworks, it is important to remember that ethnography is an approach designed to answer anthropological questions and yield ethnographic data accordingly that are fundamentally different from data collected through most other approaches. Knowledge gathering in ethnography is a dynamic *process*, in which the ethnographer is also actively involved (Blommaert & Dong, 2009a, 2010).

In this way, an ethnographic study can be considered as an archive of research, which documents the researcher's own journey through knowledge. In contrast to most other approaches, ethnography is not to simplify and reduce the complex and sometimes messy social reality, but to describe, explain and make sense of it. For an ethnographer it is not enough and often not possible to follow a clear, pre-set, linear research plan and fit it onto the social reality he or she sets to investigate; the researcher is in a mutual relation with the researched, in which both parties interact and adapt to the existence of the other one, and it is a 'relation that will change both' (Hymes, 1980: 89).

What we have seen so far, is that ethnography is designed to answer anthropological questions, is a dynamic process of knowledge gathering, and tries to capture the complexity of social actions. All these features make ethnography the right choice for this research that is essentially an anthropological inquiry into the complex processes of identity construction within a kaleidoscopic circumstance of globalisation and migration. There is one more important reason for me to follow an ethnographic approach in studying identities – what we are to find out may not be found out by asking (Hymes, 1981). Most people perform cultural and social behaviour, such as identity negotiations, without actively reflecting on it. More often than not people take things they do or things that happen to them for granted. When we see anything as normal, natural, 'that's the way it is', we usually neither have an opinion about it, nor do we turn it into an issue that can be comfortably put in words when we are asked about it. Ethnographic fieldwork, however, aims to find out things that people are often not actively aware of, things that belong to the implicit structures of their life.

My ethnographic research deploys a range of methods to find out the identity making processes that are involved in every part of our life, yet without our active awareness that this is actually something we *do*. During my fieldwork I have collected public discourses such as newspaper reports, internet downloads and government policies about migrant workers' and their children's presence in cities. These public discourses are properly ethnographic, if we consider Beijing as a huge fieldwork site and the researcher a useful tool for data collection through various means such as watching, reading and listening. I then immersed myself in a neighbourhood populated with both local urban citizens and migrants. When access to the schools became available, I spent an extended period of time in the schools, observed class sessions, communicated with pupils and teachers, and in the meantime, gave the pupils and teachers a chance to get used to my presence. Pupils' homework writing, teachers' blackboard display, and school documents were also among the data that I collected. Later in the observation, I started to interview pupils, teachers and headmasters about their perception on migrant pupils' identities. These data are organised around the scalar structure: scale 1 – linguistic and communicative exchange scale where small, everyday linguistic issues occur and carry social meanings that index identities in a bigger social context; scale 2 – metapragmatic discourse scale where people reflect and comment on migrant identities; and scale 3 – institutional and public discourse scale where rigid identity categorisations occur.

The three scales

Chapter 3 focuses on identity construction on the scale of everyday linguistic exchanges. In Chapter 3, I begin with an introduction to the central notions for data analysis of this chapter: 'space', 'scale' and 'monoglot ideology'. In the successive Chapters 4 and 5, I introduce more concepts. Together the central notions for each chapter will form the theoretical toolkit of this book. In the second part of the chapter, I present three examples. The first example demonstrates a monoglot language ideology in which Putonghua emerges as a homogeneous image that overlays the linguistic diversity. In the second example, this monoglot ideology disqualifies a migrant worker's linguistic resources as peripheral, and the peripheral accent projects a peripheral identity: the migrant identity. In the third example, a street vendor displays complicated linguistic patterns involving characteristics of three language varieties: Beijing accent, Putonghua and an accent from southern China.

Chapter 4 studies migrant identities through metapragmatic discourses and illustrate the interactions between identities made on this scale and identities constructed on the linguistic and communicative exchange scale. This chapter begins by distinguishing the notions of speech community and language community, which leads to an evaluation on the concept of ethnolinguistic identity in the complex linguistic and sociolinguistic society of China. I present four examples in this chapter. In the first example I observe a drawing class at a Beijing public primary school during which a migrant pupil articulates a metapragmatic discourse on her own and her fellow-pupils' identities. The second example is a group interview among migrant pupils about their perceptions on their own home dialects and accents. The third example shows comments of a local Beijing pupil on his migrant classmate's way of talk, and the fourth example documents a teacher's evaluations on her pupils' identity, language and performance.

I address the making of migrant identity through institutional and public discourses in Chapter 5. Public scale discourses often invoke general, generic and rigid identity categories. This chapter begins with an introduction of Foucault's notion of 'abnormality' in the sense that people who are culturally deviated from the assumed self-presentation of how *we* are, are often abnormalised by our reconstruction of their characteristics against our own categories (cf. Blommaert & Verschueren, 1998). The media and public discourses often play an active role in forming and circulating such abnormality. Other central notions of this chapter include 'stigma', 'normality' and 'modernity'. This chapter will present three examples: the first example is a periodical article on advising potential migrant workers to practise and to achieve a good proficiency of Putonghua before entering the cities. The second example documents internet debates on a news report on migrant workers in the urban space, and the third example is an interview with a school manager.

Summary

This book is an ethnography of Chinese rural–urban migrants. It is opened with a theoretical discussion on and argues for a three-scale framework, which is the central theme of this research. There have been well-established and influential approaches in the field, which have generated a great deal of research on linguistic processes of identity construction. I evaluate two major approaches of discursive studies on identity making – CA and CDA. CA emphasises the fluid, ever-changing nature of identity locally performed between participants. In contrast to CA, CDA advocates the determining role of the wider social context in the process of identity construction, which often leads to a quick interpretation of the discourse coupled with the analyst's preconceived assumptions. Both approaches, as I have argued early in this chapter, are inadequate in examining identities, particularly in today's world characterised by rapid globalisation and population movements. The ever more complex world forces us to look for and to construct analytical tools, such as the three-scale approach presented here, that do not try to reduce complexity but to accurately describe it.

The three-scale approach is illustrated through fieldwork data on internal migration processes within China. China is certainly not the only place where one can observe internal migration as part of and being conditioned by globalisation. However, the rapid re-formation in social structure and its diverse sociolinguistic landscape, along with the country's increasing participation in the World-System, offer a unique research site in studying the linguistic processes of identity construction and in exploring the usefulness of the three-scale structure in the globalised world.

This research follows the ethnographic tradition and deploys a range of methods including observation, interview and collection of written as well as electronic discourses. I establish the theoretical framework in Chapter 1. Chapter 2 will give a detailed account of the social, linguistic and methodological backgrounds. I present the three scales in the three analytical chapters: Chapters 3, 4 and 5, respectively. Finally, I draw theoretical as well as empirical conclusions in Chapter 6.

Notes

1. The Coca-Cola can metaphor is used in Blommaert (2005a) in a different way.
2. In some varieties of northern Mandarin Chinese, there is a subtle difference between *zan men* and *wo men*: both are first person plural 'we', but the former one includes both or all of the interlocutors, while the latter one often refers to the speaker and a third person or third persons who may or may not be

present in the conversation, but excludes the listener. The use of *'wo men'* signals a distance between the speaker and the hearer.
3. The latest figures are available at: http://www.stats.gov.cn/tjgb/rkpcgb/qgrkpcgb/t20060316_402310923.htm. Last accessed on 15.7.09.
4. Data source: Beijing Statistics Bureau, available at: http://www.cpirc.org.cn/news/rkxw_gn_detail.asp?id = 6574. Last accessed on 15.7.09.
5. Note that Li (2004) argues that the Nanjing dialect was the standard pronunciation until the late 18th century.

Chapter 2
A Roadmap into the Issue

Introduction

Now that we have defined the main theme of this book, let us turn to the social and methodological backgrounds of the study, so as to prepare the reader for an active engagement with the research and the arguments in the subsequent chapters. This chapter first locates the research in the wider social, sociolinguistic and institutional contexts of urban China. Second, it focuses on the ethnographic fieldwork I conducted among the internal migrants in Beijing.

The main body of this chapter is therefore split into two sections. Section 'Social and Sociolinguistic Backgrounds' sets out the background of the study, focusing on three aspects: the recent wave of internal migration as the social context, the linguistic and sociolinguistic landscapes of China and the education provision to migrant children in cities as the institutional context. The account of internal migration focuses not merely on migration itself, but also on the political, economic, social and historical settings around it. The linguistic and sociolinguistic diversity forms a necessary background for any understanding of the discursive process of constructing identities among China's internal migrants. As children of migrant workers are the major informants of the study and the two fieldwork sites are schools, I examine the education provisions to migrant children as a crucial institutional context of their identity construction.

In the section on 'Fieldwork Issues', my focus narrows down to the specific background of the fieldwork. The section begins with a theoretical discussion of the ethnographic approach at the methodological and the epistemological levels. It then documents the data history in a three-stage sequence: before, during and after fieldwork stages, and gives a detailed account of the micro-context of the field sites, the everyday rituals of the pupils and teachers, my role as a fieldworker, the observer's effects and the key incident approach as a data selection method.

Social and Sociolinguistic Backgrounds

Migration

Migration is usually seen as the phenomenon of people emigrating and immigrating, that is, people leave their place of origin and settle elsewhere for an extended period. In Western Europe, migration is traditionally concerned with transnational population movements, such as Turks and Moroccans into the Netherlands, South Asian and Caribbean people into Britain and West-Africans into France. The movements are to a large extent derived from the decolonisation processes and foreign labour policies of these host countries between the early 1950s and mid-1970s (Bezemer & Kroon, 2006; Spotti, 2007). As for China's internal migration studied in this book, the population movements occur within the country's national borders: from rural to urban areas, from the western inland to eastern coastal regions, from small towns to provincial capitals and medium-sized cities and to the metropolitan cities of Beijing, Shanghai and Guangzhou and so on. The 'super-diversity' described in urban Antwerp (Blommaert, 2009c; cf. Vertovec, 2006) can be observed in one of my fieldwork neighbourhoods in Beijing, a street that is populated with Beijing local people as well as migrant workers from diverse places. There is a dry clean shop run by a family from the North-east region, a Korean restaurant, a grocery store owned by an Anhui young man; neighbourhood cleaners, street vendors, construction workers, are all from various corners of the country. One can often guess, more or less, their place of origin from their accents. Moreover, migrant workers are diverse in term of their length of urban experience and their position in society. For example, those who have lived in Beijing for several years may become well established – they may own property (i.e. an apartment) or a business (such as a grocery shop) – whereas for new arrivals low-skilled jobs (cleaner, domestic worker, etc.) are usually their only choice. Migrant workers and local people enter into interactions on a daily basis, with their respective languages, language varieties and other cultural resources.

The scale of the internal migration is more than 10% of the country's total population, and this percentage is much higher in metropolitan areas. The migrant population counts for at least one-fifth of Beijing's total population, for instance. If the decolonisation processes and foreign labour policies gave rise to the transnational migration in Europe, what has caused China's phenomenal internal migration? The answers to this question may give us an insight into China's social structure in a transitional mode over the past decades. The drive behind the mass migration lies in rapid social and economic changes and uneven regional development. Since the launch of economic reform policies in 1978, China's gross domestic product (GDP) has been growing on average 9.4% per annum, with a six-fold increase from 1984 to 2004 (Kuijs & Wang, 2005). The average household income in 1985 was $280, and it has risen to $1290 in 2005. The United Nations Development Programme (UNDP) Millennium Development Goal (MDG) report indicated that China's MDG in poverty reduction had been achieved by halving the proportion of population living in poverty on the basis of the 85 million in 1990, 13 years ahead of schedule (UNDP, 2003). In terms of global development, China contributed at least one-third of global economic growth in 2004 (UNDP, 2005). The reform transforms the urban manufacture and services industries; however, the rural areas are further lagging behind in the country's overall booming economy.

China's rural economy was underdeveloped prior to the economic boom. When the People's Republic was established in 1949, the nation inherited an economy which was devastated by a hundred years of foreign invasion and 20 years of civil war. The economy was largely agrarian at that time, and was characterised by land scarcity and agricultural labour surplus. In order to speed up the growth of the urban industrial sector, the nation adopted several policies, the most notable one being the 'price-scissors' policy in the 1950s: the food price was kept lower than the would-be market price, so that labour cost was kept low in relation to the industrial price. This would generate high profits to be reinvested in heavy industry (cf. Knight & Song, 1999 for a fuller account). As such, wealth was transferred from the agricultural sector to capital-intensive heavy industrial sectors in cities, and farmers made less income than they would do otherwise. This policy was gradually replaced by the reforms aiming at a transition from a planned to a market economy; however, rural citizens did not benefit as much as their urban counterparts from the economic boom, and the gap between the poor and the rich has not narrowed. It has been reported that the Gini coefficient[1] of China was 40.3, which was similar to that of the United States (40.8) and the United Kingdom (36.1) (UNDP, 2003).

The rapid urbanisation and industrialisation have attracted millions of villagers to cities from rural and underdeveloped regions of the country. The informants of my study are all among this group of rural–urban migrants. Some of them have found better opportunities for life, many more are still struggling to feed themselves and their family. Before the 1980s, population movement was strictly controlled by the *hukou* household registration system. The tradition of household registration can be traced back to the Han dynasty's *bian hu zhi* (which means 'a system of synthesising everybody in term of household') and has been part of China's history for centuries. The peculiarity of the current registration is that it makes the access to social welfare and social security dependent on people's place of belonging and to people's rural or urban categorisation. Moreover, it became a marker of social status and social class, in the sense that the urban industrial working class was considered a vanguard social force, at least before the 1980s, whereas the social status of farmers had been, and is even more so now, at the lowest stratum of society. *Hukou* became an instrument of controlling population movements through the distribution of everyday supplies in the planned economy era of the 1960s and 1970s (Knight & Song, 1999). This function of tying people to their place of origin has been gradually weakened since the 1980s and migrants can move to and work in another locality without changing their household registration records. However, possessing a non-local *hukou* still means that one is not entitled to the welfare and social benefits from the local government of destination or host cities of migrants. This is particularly relevant to my study of identity construction of school-aged children in Beijing. Being a non-local *hukou* holder a migrant child is usually demarcated from his or her urban local counterparts notably by having limited access to public-funded school education, as we shall see later on in this chapter. Migrant workers, thus, become effectively a new urban proletariat, ranked lower than the local resident working class.

Voices supporting further relaxation of *hukou* are often heard and there are indeed new policy developments at regional levels.[2] Nevertheless, *hukou* is still a crucial institutional device in my empirical study. I consider the relaxation of *hukou* an important social factor that made the mass population movements possible; the essential cause of the migration, however, lies in the rapid economic growth in part of the country and the widening gap between the rich and the poor. The rural–urban divide is ever more prominent as a result of the economic boom. It, however, is not the only dimension of China's uneven development. Other dimensions include the economic contrasts between the western inland regions, such as Sichuan province, and the eastern coastal industrial areas such as Zhejiang province. Figure 2.1 shows this contrast between the vast western inland (marked in dark grey), and the eastern coastal areas (marked in mid grey: Jiangsu, Zhejiang and Guangdong provinces). The economic situations of the areas in light grey are somewhere in between. This map also shows a third dimension of the uneven development: a vertical continuum of spaces with a few metropolis such as Beijing, Tianjin, Shanghai, Shenzhen (marked also in mid grey) at one extreme, a huge number of

Figure 2.1 The uneven development of China.
Source: *China Human Development Index* for 2002. Beijing: UNDP.

towns and small cities on the other extreme and provincial capitals and medium-sized cities in between. In all three dimensions in the data analysis later on, population movements typically take place from rural to urban areas, from the western inland to the eastern coastal regions and from smaller to bigger cities. This phenomenon can be explained by Wallerstein's 'centre-periphery' analysis (Wallerstein, 2000), which we shall see in detail in Chapter 3.

All these dimensions are at the infra-state level, but bear an influence from the supra-state level. For instance, the influx of migrant workers into the eastern coastal regions reflects China's increasing participation in globalisation. The mass internal migration can be studied as part of the world labour movements, along with transnational movements of capital, information and technology, in globalisation. Thus, apart from the social and economic factors from within, globalisation and supra-state-level influences form another layer in China's internal migration. Foreign investment pours in to the coastal regions such as the Yangtze River Delta Region and the Pearl River Delta Region,[3] to take advantage of the easy seaport and airport links and cheap labour costs. The manufacturing sector of these regions surges at a startling speed – the Pearl River Delta Region alone produces nearly 5% of the world's goods, much of which is fuelled by foreign direct investment, and the products enter the overseas markets without circulation inside China. The rapidly expanding industrial and manufacturing sectors attract hundreds of thousands of labourers from inland China. Although their wage is minimal compared to what the foreign enterprises would have to pay in their own countries, the money the workers make is by all means significant compared to what they can get from tilling the land. Even if the workers' labour costs rise year by year, there is a huge reserve of young people of various educational levels from the inland who are ready to fill up vacancies. In this sense, China is positioned at a low and peripheral level in the global chain, despite its impressive export figures. This economic pattern results in a high consumption of human, natural and other resources, combined with relatively low profits: the biggest portion of profits, of course, goes to those on the higher level of the global chain, those who own the core technologies and retail channels in the West. The millions of young people, nevertheless, have a chance to leave their home villages and move to the cities for an adventure, to make a better life, and with or without awareness, to take part in the globalisation process. Consequently, the phenomenal internal migration gives rise to an ever more complex linguistic and sociolinguistic environment, and migrant workers of diverse communities relocate with their baggage of linguistic and cultural resources, interact with each other and exchange the indexical values of their regionally marked linguistic varieties.

Linguistic diversity and the standardisation of Putonghua

Linguistic diversity, rather than uniformity, is the rule in China, a nation with great cultural and linguistic diversity among its more than 50 ethnic groups (Zhou, 2005, 2006, 2007, 2008, 2009). Many ethnic groups traditionally speak their own languages, including Mongolian, Turkic and Tungus (such as Manchu) of the Altaic languages in North China; Zhuang, Dai, Kam, Li, Mulan of the Tai (*Zhuang-Dong*) languages, the Tibeto-Burman languages (such as Tibetan, Burmese, Naxi, Yi, Qiang) and the Miao-Yao languages in South China, plus many more unclassified or isolated languages such as Korean in the northeast and Bai in the south of the country (Hu, 1995). More than 30 written and nearly 100 spoken languages are officially registered to be minority languages and have official status in their respective autonomous regions. The Chinese policies encourage the use and development of minority languages in their minority areas (Zhou, 2003a). The 1954 Constitution[4] (Article 3) stipulates that every nationality has the freedom to use and develop its languages; the 1984 Autonomous Regions Law[5] (Article 21) indicates that the priority is given to the minority language when the autonomous government is dealing with ethnic minority people, even when the minority language and Putonghua (see later in this chapter) are co-official languages of an autonomous area. In an ethnic minority area, the policies are materialised, for example, through bilingual (i.e. the minority language and Putonghua) primary education and through bilingual TV programmes, broadcasting and publications.

Language choice, however, is hardly ever free from power relations and language ideology, even with the best official intention of preserving minority languages. For instance, one may function well without Putonghua in private domains within the minority region, but those who attempt to move outside their minority regions, and to move upwards in the social hierarchy, can rarely succeed without mastering Putonghua. After all, senior middle school and college education are mostly accessible in Putonghua, and this language choice tacitly excludes to a large extent those who only speak minority language or dialect. It is hardly surprising that the linguistic landscapes of minority languages are gradually changing within the wider social context of mass internal population movements.

The minority languages stand face-to-face with the 'Chinese language'. The term 'Chinese' (*Zhongwen* or *Hanyu*) often refers to the language spoken by ethnic Han Chinese, although some scholars argue that it should cover all languages spoken in China, including the ethnic minority languages. In this book, I use 'Chinese' as an umbrella term to cover various dialects and varieties that share a common writing system, literature and a common history. Linguists often distinguish seven major dialects: *Guan* (Mandarin, typified by Beijing dialects), *Wu* (typified by Shanghainese), *Xiang, Gan, Kejia* (also known as Hakka among Cantonese speakers), *Min* (including the Taiwanese variety) and *Yue* (also known as Cantonese) (Chen, 1999; De Francis, 1984; Hu, 1995; Kratochvil, 1968; Ramsey, 1987; Zhang, 2002).

The debate of whether the many varieties should rather be studied as separated languages has been in the field as least since the time of Leonard Bloomfield (whose views were later challenged by Wang Li, a Chinese linguist in the 20th century). The degree of diversity among Chinese dialects is analogous to that of the European languages of the Roman family: The differences between Beijing Mandarin and Chaozhou vernacular are not less than those between Italian and French (Norman, 1988). The language versus dialect debate lies in the fundamentally different definitions of 'dialect' between the Chinese tradition and the western tradition. 'Mutual intelligibility' serves as the central criterion in the western tradition,[6] whereas common orthography, shared literature, historical roots, cultural heritage and political unity, play a decisive role in labelling a variety as a 'dialect' or a 'language' in the Chinese tradition. Consequently, what in the Western tradition would be seen as difference between languages (e.g. Spanish, French and Italian) would in the Chinese tradition be seen as difference between dialects (Kratochvil, 1968: 15–16; Ramsey, 1987: 17–18).

No matter which definition of 'dialect' one follows, the degree of linguistic diversity within the Chinese language is not to be underestimated. In such linguistically complex environments, Putonghua represents yet another layer of complexity. It is a standardised form of Mandarin spoken in Beijing and its nearby regions. The established view holds that there was no unified pronunciation in China until the early 20th century (e.g. Norman, 1988; Ramsey, 1987). The linguistic standard prior to that is said to be the written Classical Chinese which, perhaps the oldest script in the world, had been in uninterrupted use for over 2000 years (Chen, 1999; Guo & Gao, 2003).

The modern Putonghua is closely related to Mandarin, the 'language of the officials' of the Yuan (1260 AD–1368 AD), Ming (1368 AD–1644 AD) and Qing (1644 AD–1912 AD) dynasties, the so-called 'Mandarins' in early European missionary expressions (Coblin, 2000). The prevalent view among both linguists and lay persons is that Mandarin has been very similar to, if not exactly identical with, the language of Beijing over approximately 800 years. Recent research challenges this view and argues that 'for most of its history standard Mandarin had little to do with Pekinese' (Coblin, 2000: 537). According to Coblin, the Beijing-based pronunciation was rejected by intellectuals and officials as Altaicised 'Tartar-Chinese', a stigmatised variety with characteristics of the northern nomadic languages. Instead of Beijing Mandarin, it is argued that the Nanjing-based pronunciation was the standard Mandarin until at least the late 18th century (Li, 2004).

How did a once alien and stigmatised language gain ground, and how did it eventually replace the then official pronunciation? It is now safe to say that the two varieties of Mandarin (i.e. the Beijing-based versus the Nanjing-based) co-existed and competed against each other for some time before the late 18th century, and the Beijing-based Mandarin finally prevailed in a gradual but dramatic phonological shift (Dong, 2010a). It is important to note that Mandarin is neither a singular entity nor a language with linear development; rather, it was and is polycentric and multifaceted.

Its enregisterment as the official language of the Mandarins in the late 18th century testified to not only the competition between the two varieties but also the power relations between the political groups (Dong, 2010a).

Mandarin had been the language of feudal officials in the imperial court for centuries. It was, however, never a national language. The search for a national language was felt urgently in the late 19th and the early 20th century, an era of social and political transition from an 'old', 'backward' feudal China to a new and 'modern' state. The belief of the connection between a unified national language and national strength was convincingly presented by those colonial powers that then occupied China. France, England, Germany, Russia and Japan all had well-defined national languages (Ramsey, 1987: 4), although the formation of truly hegemonic national languages was only a 19th-century process. *Guoyu*, the immediate predecessor of Putonghua, was launched in 1926 soon after the Nationalists overthrew the feudal Qing dynasty and seized power. *Guoyu* was defined as 'the pronunciation of *educated* natives of Beijing', or of elite Beijing accent, to be the national standard (Li, 2004: 103). This definition is largely shared by Putonghua which 'is modelled on the pronunciation of Beijing, draws on Northern Chinese as its base dialect, and receives its syntactic norms from exemplary works of contemporary vernacular literature' (Hu, 1987: 15), defined in 1955 and revised in 1956 by the People's Republic. Note that the word 'educated' in the 1926 definition disappeared here, due to anti-bourgeois sentiments following the success of the Communist Revolution (Li, 2004) Instead, the language of grassroots 'ordinary people', or common speech, characterises the new standard pronunciation with a democratic aspiration similar to Swahili as 'the language of the people' in Tanzania (Blommaert, 1999).

Putonghua is often understood as a phonological standard, but it also has a syntactic and lexical dimension. As its 1956 definition indicates, Putonghua 'receives its syntactic norms from exemplary works of contemporary vernacular literature'. The 'vernacular literature', known as *Baihuawen* (literally 'unadorned Chinese'), is the modern standard written Chinese. It emerged around the Tang dynasty (618–907 AD), and replaced Classical Chinese (*Wenyanwen*) as the written standard in the 1920s and the 1930s (Chen, 1999). The difference between *Baihuawen* and *Wenyanwen*, to put it very briefly, lies in that the former is close to spoken Mandarin, whereas the latter, although considered as 'refined' and 'elegant', is largely divorced from speaking. People might speak in dramatically different dialects, but in the formal domains such as education and administration, they had used *Wenyanwen* as a common written medium until the early 20th century. Some regional vernaculars, particularly Wu, Min, Yue

(Cantonese), do have written forms developed to various degrees, but they are mostly confined within the domain of popular culture and are generally held to be of low prestige. By the 1950s, along with the standardisation of Putonghua, *Baihuawen* served as the syntactic basis of the standardisation of Putonghua. Although this syntactic and lexical dimension is involved occasionally, in this study I mainly see Putonghua as a phonological phenomenon.

The linguistic diversity and the sociolinguistic evolvement of standard Putonghua sketched here serve as important backgrounds of my research. The discursive process of migrant identity construction is positioned in such a diverse and complex linguistic context. The languages as well as dialects used by migrant workers and their children are in daily interactions with those of local urban citizens, and in particular, with standard Putonghua. In the country's formal education domain, where the majority of my data collection took place, Putonghua is the language of instruction. In order to understand the making of identities among migrant children, we shall take a look at the institutional context of urban education, particularly migrant children's access to urban public schooling, in the next section.

Education provision to migrant children

Among China's 150 million internal migrants, children form a young but important subgroup, as their education and living conditions have caused much public concern and media debate. The common concern is that urban public primary and secondary schools have inadequate capacity to accommodate the influx of migrant children, and therefore migrant parents have either to pay higher fees for their children to be admitted at public schools, or to send them to privately run migrant schools. Some parents have to leave their children to their relatives or boarding schools in their hometown because they find the living and schooling costs of their children in cities unaffordable. Debates over migrant children's education are centred on two issues: (1) who should pay for their education, and (2) what is the role of privately run migrant schools. This section describes the migrant children's position in China's education system through addressing these two issues.

Who should pay for a child's compulsory education?[7] Definitely the state. The answer is simple, but at ground level, things are a good deal more complicated. Who pays for children's education determines where they are entitled to free or subsidised schooling. China's Compulsory Education Law says that regional governments (i.e. city districts, towns and villages) are responsible for the compulsory education of the children in their administration areas. Three bodies finance a child's compulsory education: the central government, the regional government and the child's family.[8] Both central and regional governments' funds are allocated through the regional government to the public school according to the number of school-aged *hukou* children in the school's neighbourhood area. Note that this is not the number of children the school admits, nor children who reside in the area, but *hukou* children who have their household registration in the area. Recall what we know about *hukou* from section 'Migration': Possessing a local *hukou* means that one is entitled to welfare and social benefits from the local government. As most migrant workers move into cities without having their *hukou* changed,[9] the government budget for migrant children's education still goes to the schools of their hometown, that is, the school of the neighbourhood where their *hukou* is registered. This is why an early policy concerning migrant children issued in 1998[10] said that the local government of a migrant's *hukou* locality should prevent children of migrant workers from migration. This policy means that every child should attend schools in their *hukou* neighbourhood, as long as a legal guardian is available (Dong, 2010b).

It was soon proved unpractical and impossible to have a child separated from the parents for a long period. In order for their children to have formal and quality education, migrant parents were often required to pay higher fees than the children of local *hukou*-holders by urban public schools, on grounds that the school did not receive subsidy from the local government for a pupil without local *hukou*, and the higher fees were to make up for the portion of the local government's subsidy. The higher fees were often unaffordable for migrant workers who on average had a lower income than their urban working class counterparts. To meet the surging demand of schooling for migrant children, privately run migrant schools emerged in the early 1990s. It is believed that their original drive was simple: Migrant workers spontaneously set up schools, or more precisely, private classes and tutoring, because their children had no schools to go to. A headmaster of one of the earliest migrant schools saw 'children running wild in vegetable plots and romping beside their parents' vegetable stalls; even fifteen-year-old children had no school to go to' (Han, 2001: 4). She thus decided to set up a school so that the children from her hometown would have a chance to read and write. Because of the large demand from migrant families, her school expanded rapidly and admitted pupils not only from her hometown but also from almost every province of the country. This case reported in Han (2001) was typical of how migrant schools emerged and developed in the early 1990s.

These early migrant schools were quickly converted into enterprises, because of the new business opportunities of meeting the demands for education from migrant populations, and the number of such schools increased dramatically in the 1990s. In China's education system, government-funded public schools are the major education provider, and there is a growing number of private elite schools offering expensive education services. However, the privately run 'migrant schools' we are talking about here are not among such elite schools. On the contrary, the facilities and teaching of such schools were generally poor. To operate on lower fees than those of subsidised public schools and still make a profit, migrant schools had to compromise school conditions and teaching quality (Han, 2001; Lu & Zhang, 2001; Woronov, 2004; Zhang et al., 2003; Zou et al., 2005). With a few exceptions where the proprietors were able to invest in property, most schools were built in temporary classrooms or rented cheap spaces such as warehouses that might have no windows; the lighting and ventilation was often poor; blackboards were made from pieces of wood painted with black paint; pupils' desks and chairs were of various sizes in one classroom, while some schools even 'improvised' desks and chairs from wooden planks propped up on bricks (Han, 2001: 6). Classrooms were often over-crowded. In the sample of Han (2001), 11% of the classes had more than 70 pupils, and there was a class packed with 84 children. Many schools had no playground and their pupils had to have their physical exercise class in the street.

The description in Han (2001) was about migrant schools 8 or 10 years back; my fieldwork visits to many migrant schools between 2006 and 2009 showed that increasingly more migrant children made their way to public schools, and that not every migrant school was still poorly equipped. Nevertheless, problems remain. For example, teaching quality was a major concern, because many migrant schools, willingly or not, employed unqualified teaching staff to keep costs low. Qualified teachers who were by no means many in these schools were often very mobile – they tended to see the teaching post as a temporary 'springboard' and would readily leave it for a better job. The frequent change of teachers had at least two unfavourable impacts on pupils: first, the teaching tended to be inconsistent. Second, they were discouraged by their teachers' attitudes towards pupils and pupils' academic careers.

Policy-makers were aware of the unrealistic attempt to discourage children from migrating, as well as the potential negative impacts of underachieving migrant schools on pupils' development. More importantly, migrant children were effectively segregated from their local counterparts and the mainstream urban communities by the way the education system functioned. They might be stigmatised by having to attend these 'second-class' schools, and mutual mistrust might grow between urban and migrant children who had little chance to get to know one another. A series of policies were devised to ensure migrant children's right of education in cities and to regulate privately run migrant schools. For example, the 1997 regulation[11] governed the standards of privately run migrant schools; the 2001 regulation[12] stipulated that public schools in cities should be the major education provider to migrant children; and the regulations issued in 2003[13] said that migrant children should pay the same tuition fees as local pupils and public schools should reduce or waive fees of migrant children if necessary (Dong, 2010b). Cities such as Beijing vowed to accommodate most migrant children within the publicly funded education system and to close down underachieving migrant schools. This ambition, however, is not easy to achieve. One of the reasons that discourages migrant children from joining public schools is the concern of being discriminated by their urban peer students and teachers. Many migrant children in my fieldwork schools indicated that they believed their regional accents would (in the case of migrant middle school) or did (in the case of public primary school) differentiate them from local Beijing pupils whose speech they perceived to be 'accent-less'.

A more determining reason is that, from a macro level, urban public schools have to enlarge and increase their capacities to accommodate the huge number of migrant pupils whose education costs are not covered by public subsidy. Regulations have been devised but these regulations are rarely backed up by financial support, that is, the regulations only say that urban government should educate migrant children in their administrative areas, without saying how much funding they would receive to implement the task. In short, although more and more migrant children join public schools with their urban peer students, and one of the fieldwork sites in my research is such a public school, migrant children's education in cities remains a social concern, a reflection of a transitional society in which inequality occurs along with the making and remaking of new social and class fractions.

I conducted my fieldwork in these wider social, sociolinguistic and institutional backgrounds of mass labour migration within the country, intense linguistic exchanges among various communities, and the education concerns of migrant children in cities as well as their interaction with local urban children. So far we have dealt with rather general information of the research at a macro and societal level; let us now turn to ethnography – the methodological background of the present research.

Fieldwork Issues

This section focuses on the experience of carrying out ethnographic fieldwork in the migrant communities of urban Beijing between 2006 and 2009. Before narrowing our gaze to the fieldwork sites and the data collection, a brief account of some basic but fundamental understandings of ethnography is in order. Therefore, this methodological section is comprised of two parts: a theoretical discussion on ethnography, and a description of the fieldwork journey.[14]

Ethnography and language study

Ethnography is often seen as a research method for collecting particular types of data, sometimes as another name for description, or even something that can be said about 'context'. In such discussions, talk is sometimes separated from its context, and whereas the study of talk is a task for linguistics, CA or discourse analysis, the study of context is a matter for ethnography. It is against this narrow view that I position my argument of ethnography here: rather than a matter of description, ethnography can be seen as a full intellectual programme that involves a perspective on language and communication, including an ontology and an epistemology, both of which are essential for the study of language in society.

To understand ethnography, we have to understand its history, a history that reveals its intellectual origins inscribed in its techniques and patterns of operation. Ethnography has its origin in anthropology. That means that ethnography contains ontologies, methodologies and epistemologies situated within the tradition of anthropology. 'It is anthropology's task to coordinate knowledge about language from the viewpoint of *man*' (Hymes, 1964: xiii), which means that language is studied as something that has a certain relevance to humanity, and humanity in anthropology is seen as closely linked, conditioned or determined by society, community, the group and culture. One important consequence of this anthropological background to ethnography is the ontology, the definition of language itself. Language, in this tradition, is seen as a socially loaded and assessed tool for humans, which enables humans to perform as social beings, a resource to be used by human beings in social life, means available to human beings in societies. These resources can be deployed in various circumstances, but when this happens it never happens in a neutral way. Every act of language use is an act that is assessed, weighed and measured socially.

This view of language leads to the epistemological level of ethnography. Knowledge of language facts is processual and historical; this lifts single language acts to a level of relevance much higher than language acts, which in turn become indexical of wider dimensions and contexts, and these wider dimensions are part of ethnographic interpretation. Fabian stresses the dynamic process of knowledge gathering in ethnography, emphasising that ethnographic work also entails active involvement from the ethnographer himself. This provides ethnography with a peculiar, dynamic and dialectical epistemology in which the *ignorance* of the knower – the ethnographer – is a crucial point of departure (Fabian, 1995). Consequently, ethnography attributes great importance to the history of what is commonly seen as 'data': the whole process of gathering and moulding knowledge is part of that knowledge; knowledge construction is knowledge, the process is the product (see Blommaert, 2001, 2004; Ochs, 1979).

To summarise, the anthropological roots are central to ethnography, which situates language deeply in social life and offers a distinct ontology and epistemology to ethnography. Language in ethnography is something very different from what it is in many other branches of the languages sciences, and so is the status of gathering knowledge. As a consequence, the next section describes my fieldwork journey of gathering and moulding knowledge of language use among migrant workers and their children in Beijing.

Data history

Ethnographic fieldwork produces an archive of research, and this archive documents the researcher's own journey of knowledge construction. Fieldwork journey is a crucial learning process to every fieldworker; unfortunately, it often disappears in most ethnographic accounts. This section therefore provides such an archive on my fieldwork journey. For the sake of clarity, this section is organised in the sequence of three stages: prior to fieldwork, during fieldwork and after fieldwork. However, each stage comprises several sub-parts, and these sub-parts are often overlapping and simultaneous, whereas the three stages are necessarily sequential.

The stage *prior to fieldwork* involves two major activities: preparation and documentation. Preparation starts as soon as one begins research, develops an interest in a particular topic or field, and works on a proposal. It often entails reading of a good deal of theoretically and methodologically informative works, which helps direct the researcher's attention to particular phenomena and aspects of social reality. At a certain point of preparation, the researcher has to decide whether to include ethnographic fieldwork. The decision for ethnographic fieldwork means that the researcher has to subscribe to the general epistemological and methodological principles of ethnographic studies: The research results cannot claim to be representative, it will not be replicable under identical circumstances, nor will it claim to produce 'uncontaminated' evidence and so on. Instead, it is interpretive research in a situated, real environment, based on interaction between the researcher and the researched, hence, fundamentally subjective in nature, aimed at describing complexity, and yielding hypotheses that can be replicated and tested in similar, but not identical, circumstances. This decision is part of the learning process.

Having decided on the ethnographic approach to fieldwork, my main task for fieldwork preparation was to understand and study the possible macro- as well as micro-contexts in which the fieldwork would occur. For the study of migrant children's identity construction, macro-contexts involved historical, political, institutional, social structural and cultural aspects around the issue of internal migration, whereas micro-contexts included changeable, accidental, unpredictable contexts that defined the situation. The task of understanding the macro-contexts was fulfilled through collecting documents on government policies, media reports and academic research reports. The intensive documentary research took about five months prior to my departure for the field, whereas the access to the special archives in China's national library had to be done on entering the field.

In addition to documentation, a crucial task I accomplished in the preparation stage was to build up initial contacts with established Chinese researchers from the field of migration studies. We corresponded via internet for half a year prior to my fieldwork, and the researchers not only provided me with useful insights on the research topic, but also agreed to help with the access to migrant schools. I was then almost ready for fieldwork.

The stage *during fieldwork* was, however, chaotic and unpredictable. The first surprise I had to face is that my contacts happened to be away from Beijing and were unreachable by any modern communication means. I therefore decided to conduct some carpet-searching and mobilised everybody I knew to look for accessible migrant schools. Fortunately, several migrant schools were found, and I decided to negotiate my access with the headmasters for conducting research in their schools. Most headmasters refused my request bluntly; only one of them had a little chat with me and confided that no migrant school would let me in because the local government was determined to close down those privately run migrant schools that could not satisfy the safety, hygiene and teaching standards set out by the local government, and according to him, less than 10% of such schools could reach the standards. It turned out to be an unfortunate time to seek access to migrant schools when headmasters were afraid and suspicious of any stranger. I thus set off looking for and successfully found a migrant school officially recognised by the local educational authority that should not be in fear of being closed down. However, the headmaster was very careful with getting involved in any research because it was hard for the school to be recognised and he did not want to do anything that might upset the local educational authority. I could do fieldwork in his school only if I held a recommendation from the local educational authority. After many twists and turns, I had a chance to meet officials from the local educational authority and to present my research plan, which appeared to interest the officials; they needed time to consider the proposal. The consideration, however, seemed to take forever. Almost three months passed in the search-and-wait mode. I took solace from Nigel Barley's experience:

> Fieldwork seems to consist of long periods that are impossible to reconstruct afterwards because nothing happened, alternating with days of intense activity when one rides a rollercoaster of good fortune and disaster. (Barley, 1987: 60)

It was a period of deep frustration, disappointment and confusion, in which nothing seemed to happen. I had to look elsewhere for research opportunities before school access worked out; to encounter and manage small talks with migrant workers in streets seemed a plausible solution, and this is the origin of the street corner data in Chapter 3, which turned out to be an informative case on identity construction at the scale of linguistic interaction. I include the searching of fieldwork sites in the *during fieldwork* stage, rather than the *prior to fieldwork* stage, because it was part of the learning process: as a fieldworker, I by definition arrived as an outsider, although Beijing is my place of origin. The preparation had provided useful knowledge, but such tacit codes as the fear of being closed down was hardly predictable from preparation.

The good luck began when my contacts returned. Through their connections I quickly got access to a privately run migrant junior middle school. The founders of this school were among the very first ones who set up private migrant schools in the early 1990s. It was initially a small primary school with only two staff – the founder and his wife, and some 15 pupils; with the huge demand of schooling from migrant communities, their school quickly expended into hundreds of pupils and had to split into several branches. Now the enterprise was further expanded into a boarding junior middle school for migrant students. The local authority had recognised the primary school and its branches, but this was not the case of the middle school. My role was a voluntary teacher of a grade 7 class and I taught English three times a week. In return, I could freely interview the teachers, students, tape my class sessions and participate in school activities such as term-end celebration; I was not allowed to sit in and do class observation. I stayed in the middle school three days a week.

Soon after, a second fieldwork site – a public primary school – became available. It was an unexpected gain from a telephone chat with an old friend of mine; her sister turned out to be a teacher at the public school that admitted both local and migrant pupils. We talked about my research and she promised to try and see whether her headmaster would be interested. A few days later she came back with the positive response that I could do research in their school; in return I should offer teacher training sessions. I therefore visited the public school two days a week for class observation and interviews, with an extra afternoon every other week to hold teacher-training seminars. The public primary school was an ideal site to observe interaction between migrant children and their local urban peer-students as well as to interview the teachers for their evaluation on migrant pupils.

The longer I stayed in the schools, the less the observer's effect became an issue. However, there is always an observer's effect. A fieldworker rarely belongs 'naturally' to the field she investigates, but is always a foreign body – when she enters a classroom, the whole classroom changes, and a lot of what the fieldworker will witness are reactions, adjustments and adaptations to this change. It is essential for a fieldworker to realise that: she never observes an event as if she was not there. The fieldworker is there, and that makes it a different event. The observer's effect was obvious at the beginning of my fieldwork in the public primary school – the headmaster was keen to do research and asked me to set up and to lead a research team of four teachers plus the headmaster herself, insisting that the research team should do class observation with me. It is not hard to imagine how the class looked with six observers sitting at the back and watching: the teachers were nervous, students quiet, classes rehearsed. In the first few days the observation was fruitless – what we observed was miles away from what it usually was. The four teacher researchers quickly dropped out because of their teaching duties, and the headmaster stopped class observation about a month later. By then the teachers and pupils had been familiar with my presence and the fieldwork started yielding rich data from observation of the interactions between migrant and local Beijing pupils, as well as from interviews of teachers and pupils on their evaluation of accent and identity.

This *during fieldwork* stage took around 11 months, of which the first three months or so were spent on searching for accessible schools as well as collecting street corner data; the rest of this period, except for school holidays, I was in fieldwork sites at least five days a week, three days in the migrant junior middle school and two days in the public primary school. The 'products' of fieldwork include hundreds of pages of fieldnotes, around 40 hours of audio-taped conversations and interviews, copies of pupils' homework, photos of class and school activities, classroom displays, teachers' blackboard displays, two questionnaires – one is on the teachers' evaluation of pupil performance and the other on migrant parents' opinions of their children's schooling – and booklets of school regulation and so on. I was then loaded with fieldwork data and decided to proceed to the next stage – the *after fieldwork* stage.

Obviously, in the *after fieldwork* stage, one tends to do different things than in the *during fieldwork* stage. Yet, the boundary between the *during fieldwork* stage and *after fieldwork* stage was not clear-cut, because much of the interpretation of the data had already been done in the field, on a daily basis, while I was trying to make sense of the data. Another reason that the *after fieldwork* stage could not be clearly distinguished from the *during fieldwork* stage was that the learning process continued even when I stopped visiting the fieldwork sites. For example, preparing data, especially going through and transcribing audio-recorded interviews, was part of the learning process and was an extremely humbling task: to listen to myself as the interviewer hastening to the next topic, or talking while I should have remained silent so as to leave more room to the interviewee, producing a comment that was not particularly encouraging, or *too* 'encouraging' (even misleading) for the interviewee to give an answer that I might subconsciously hope for and so forth. The reflexive activities on recorded interviews could not be left to the *after fieldwork* stage, but was a continuous job, for a fieldworker must go through recordings at the earliest possible time to know what could be improved next time or next day (I give a summary of the fieldwork archives in Appendix 1).

The main task of the *after fieldwork* stage is to prepare data for further analysis and interpretation. The data are organised systematically alone the line of the 'key incident approach' (Bezemer, 2003; Erickson, 1977; Green & Bloome, 1997; Kroon & Sturm, 2007; Spotti, 2007; Wilcox, 1980). The key incident approach, according to Erickson

> to pull out from field notes a key incident, link it to other incidents, phenomena, and theoretical constructs, and write it up so others can see the generic in the particular, the universal in the concrete, the relation between part and whole. (Erickson, 1977: 61, cited in Bezemer, 2003: 30)

In other words, the key incident approach is to identify microscopic incidents that link to other incidents and that index issues at bigger, higher and macro levels. An incident is counted as 'key', says Wilcox, 'in that it represents concrete instances of the working of abstract principles of social organization' (Wilcox, 1980: 9). These include recurrent events and incidents that have sustaining influence (Green & Bloome, 1997: 186). Kroon and Sturm (2007) give an example of the key incident approach by presenting an observation of a spelling lesson to primary school pupils in a Dutch case study. The incident, although of limited nature, is placed in relation to other incidents of the research project, and together they point to general tendencies of language education in the Dutch social context and beyond. In the present study, the data selection is conducted according to the key incident approach to make it a sound and salient selection and to strike a balance between different types of data.

Summary

This chapter addresses the social, sociolinguistic, institutional and methodological backgrounds of the research. The social context is the phenomenal migration within China that began in the early 1980s and continues to this day. The internal migration is an important social background for the study of discursive identity construction, as it results in more intensive linguistic exchanges among various communities in China as well as more complicated sociolinguistic environments. The linguistic landscape of China has always been complex. The classification and description of China's languages and dialects cannot be read as reducing language to be a static and unchangeable property; rather, languages and language varieties are seen as resources ordered and stratified in a polyglot linguistic repertoire. The institutional backgrounds of my study are the education provisions for children of migrant families. In this chapter, I question the educational difficulties of migrant children in the urban areas and explore the origins and situations of privately run migrant schools. Migrant pupils' linguistic features, together with other factors, may act as an active marker for differentiating them from local 'accentless' Beijing pupils in school contexts.

I conducted my ethnographic fieldwork in these complex social, sociolinguistic and institutional contexts. The second part of this chapter argues that ethnography has to be considered as a full intellectual programme rooted in anthropological origins. At the ontological level, language is seen as a socially loaded and assessed tool for humans, a social and culturally embedded resource to be used by human beings in social life. At the epistemological level, knowledge of language facts is processual and historical, of which single language acts are lifted to and become indexical of wider dimensions and contexts. Consequently, the whole process of gathering and moulding knowledge is part of that knowledge. Having looked at the social and methodological contexts, we shall continue to the analytical chapters (Chapters 3, 4 and 5), which present and analyse fieldwork data within the three-scale framework proposed in Chapter 1. The next chapter, Chapter 3, deals with migrant identity making on the linguistic and communicative exchange scale.

Notes

1. The Gini index measures inequality over the entire distribution of income or consumption. A value of 0 represents perfect equality, and a value of 100 perfect inequality. It is believed that there can be social tensions if the Gini coefficient exceeds 40.0.
2. Metropolises such as Beijing, Shanghai, Guangzhou have new policies of granting *hukou* to 'technology immigrants' who possess special skills that fit into the fast-growing economic sectors.
3. The Yangtze River Delta generally comprises the triangular-shaped territory of Shanghai, southern Jiangsu province and northern Zhejiang province of China; the Pearl River Delta covers the low-lying areas alongside the Pearl River estuary, Hong Kong and Macau.
4. The 1954 Constitute is available at: http://news.xinhuanet.com/ziliao/2004-02/18/content_1320274.htm. Last accessed on 15.7.09.
5. The Central People's Government of the People's Republic of China: http://www.gov.cn/test/2005-07/29/content_18338.htm. Last accessed on 15.7.09.
6. Recent criticism of the intelligibility criterion argues that mutual intelligibility may ultimately depend on such extra-linguistic factors as exposure and experience (Li, 2004).
7. China has a nine-year compulsory education system that covers from primary school to junior secondary school, about age 6–15.
8. The policy of completely free compulsory education has been implemented in some rural areas and cities are gradually moving towards it.

9. It is usually extremely difficult to change one's *hukou* from rural to urban categories, or from smaller cities to bigger cities.
10. *Provisional Regulations on Schooling for Migrant Children*, issued by the National Education Committee and the Ministry of Public Security of China in 1998. The National Education Committee is today's China Ministry of Education.
11. *Regulations on Running Private School*, issued by the State Council in 1997.
12. *Decisions on Reform and Development of Basic Education*, issued by China's State Council in 2001.
13. *The Notice about Managing and Providing Services to Migrant Workers in Urban Areas*, issued by China's State Council in January 2003; *Instructions on Further Improving Compulsory Education Provision to Migrant Children in Urban Areas*, in September 2003.
14. In the following section, I draw from Blommaert and Dong (2010).

Chapter 3
Scale 1: Interaction

Introduction

Having established the general theoretical framework of this study in Chapter 1, and the social contexts as well as methodological background in Chapter 2, I examine the discursive process of establishing migrant identities on the lowest scale – the scale of everyday linguistic exchanges in this chapter. The three-scale general framework is an analytical tool that suggests a way of understanding identity construction as a multilayered object: on the scale of local linguistic interaction, identities are fluid and ever changing; on a higher scale, that is, on the metapragmatic discourse scale, identities are not only inhabited by oneself but ascribed by the evaluation of others; on the top scale identities become more rigid and abstract than those on the two lower scales, and labels such as nationality, ethnicity and gender are in many cases stable categories.[1]

In what follows, I begin with a discussion on the 'central' notions of this chapter – 'space', 'scale' and 'monoglot ideology'. Chapters 4 and 5 also begin with theoretical discussions on central notions, followed by elaboration and application of those notions in data analysis. In the second half of this chapter, I use the central notions of this chapter in three examples to illustrate identity construction on the linguistic and communicative exchange scale.

Central Concepts: Space, Scale and Monoglot Ideology
Scale and space

'Scale' is the core element of the vertical and stratified structure of identity construction that I have established in Chapter 1. In this chapter, the notion of scale, in line with its application as a spatiotemporal metaphor throughout the book, specifically refers to a spatiotemporal scope that explains the indexical nature of space and time that are ordered and organised in a vertical continuum. The notion of scale has been developed and was deployed in several disciplines including history, human geography, urban studies and anthropology (cf. Harvey, 2001; Lefebvre, 2003; Swyngedouw, 1996; Uitermark, 2002; Wallerstein, 1983, 2000, 2001), before its extension into sociolinguistic domains (Blommaert, 2005a, 2005b, 2006a; Blommaert *et al.*, 2005a, 2005b). It is easy to see 'scale' as a spatial notion; however, it has a temporal dimension that is often overlooked. In what follows, I address this concept first from its spatial aspect and second from its temporal aspect.

If we approach 'scale' as a spatial concept, we can distinguish, from Henri Lefebvre's works in the urban studies sphere, a construction of levels and dimensions, comprising the global level (G), the mixed level (M) and the private level (P), theorised in the French context (Lefebvre, 2003). The global level, according to Lefebvre, is defined as an institutional space in which the State and its political power operate. Lefebvre calls the mixed level as the level of 'city', or 'the level in between', referring to a mixture of those belonging to the global level, such as ministry buildings and cathedrals, and those belonging to the private level, for example, private buildings. The private level is the level of 'habitation', blocks of flats, detached houses, shanty towns and so on. Lefebvre's arguments of the state as spatially organised at the scales of local, national and international are taken on board by David Harvey and later Erik Swyngedouw. Swyngedouw's (1996) social geographic case study on the closing of Belgian mines in the 1980s demonstrates a 're-scaling' process of the state as part of a wider and more globally presented restructuring of the political economy. He concludes that the way in which the regional space is reconfigured into a more competitive place in the world economy is characterised by the 're-scaling' of the state, that is, the more prominent role of governance at both local and supra-national level, and the rise of 'glocal' state – the elite coalitions between the political and financial forces at both the local and the supra-national levels. In a summary of the recent re-scaling and scalar organisation literature, Uitermark (2002) cites Swyngedouw (1996) and argues that spatial scale is not something pre-given, but a process that is always contested and temporal, and appears to be the outcome of social struggles for power and control. Illustrated with evidence form the Netherlands, Uitermark (2002) proposes that every instance of 'jumping scales' presupposes the capacities of performing such a move. Whereas some have the capacity, others do not. Furthermore, a power increase of those who can jump scales is often at the expense of those who cannot, those who are trapped in their space (Swyngedouw, 1996; Uitermark, 2002). A simple example may illustrate this: one is empowered by possessing a car and being able to shop in suburban supermarkets; however, this leads to the rising prices in the neighbourhood grocery stores, and so in turn disempowers those who have less mobility and rely on such small stores.

Jumping scales, therefore, involves not only a move across space but also the different degrees to which people have control over such flows and movement – 'power geometry', as it is called by Massey (1994). There are people who have more control over the moves than others, people who can initiate and shape such flows of movement, as well as people who are on the receiving end of it, and people who are practically imprisoned by it. In short, people and social groups are positioned in different relations to the flows and interconnections. In theorising a 'global sense of place', Massey describes Kilburn High Road in North-West London where one could buy Indian saris, chat with a Muslim newsagent, while having to be interrupted by aeroplanes carrying passengers from another continent flying just overhead. The sketch of Kilburn High Road, an ordinary neighbourhood in London, inevitably brings into play almost half of the world (what is particular here, as Massey points out, is perhaps the considerable role of British imperialist history that not every country shares) that invokes a 'global sense of place'.

These recent theorisations of scale as a spatial scope in various fields of the social sciences are important for the development of the notion in sociolinguistics, and such theoretical development in sociolinguistics also contributes to wider discussions about scale and space (Blommaert, 2005a, 2005b, 2006a). The concept is formed within a language ideologies framework (notably Blommaert, 2005a; Silverstein, 2004). In this and related work, space is seen not just as a neutral background but as agentive in sociolinguistic processes. People who are highly linguistically competent may feel incapable of performing basic communicative tasks such as asking for directions and catching a taxi when they are in a foreign country, or indeed in a place where the linguistic conditions are noticeably different. Such communicative problems occur not because these people lack the competence to communicate or interact *per se*, but because the space, which organises patterns of language in particular ways, has changed (Dong & Blommaert, 2009). Such a change of space results in a mismatch between one's linguistic repertoire and the linguistic competence required in that space, and therefore incapacitates one in some communicative events (Blommaert *et al.*, 2005a).

Space, therefore, is not neutral from the moment social beings act in and on it. People speak in and from a space that projects particular social values, social order, authority and affective attributes (Blommaert, 2005b;

Scollon & Scollon, 2003). In such a space people take different positions and orient towards the topics and the interlocutors by systematically organising the patterns of speech, and therefore construct their identities in the performative process through social and linguistic interactions (Blommaert, 2005a; Butler, 1990; Goffman, 1974a, 1981). Thus, through social action, space is not passive, but constitutive in shaping the way people connect to one another, in shifting linguistic patterns and styles towards particular topics, and hence in inhabiting as well as ascribing individual identities in interaction. People maintain their language competence, or even expand their linguistic repertoires and improve their communicative skills, but because they are 'out of place' and travel across spaces, they are incapacitated and experience the changes of value attached to certain linguistic resources and patterns, value of the prestige or the stigmatised, the high or the low, the 'good' language or the 'bad' language.

Therefore, a space is meaningful in relation to another space; spaces are ordered and organised, layered and stratified, and processes belonging to one scale enter processes at another scale (Blommaert, 2005a: 23). The notion of 'scale' introduces a *vertical* spatial metaphor into sociolinguistics: an image of a continuum on which spaces are hierarchically stratified and ordered from local to global with intermediary levels between the two poles (Blommaert, 2006a). As we have seen, the vertical move from one scale to another, from local to translocal, from momentary to timeless, from individual to stereotype, from specific to general, involves and presupposes access to particular resources, and such access is often subject to power and inequality. The notion of scale is developed as a critical extension of traditional horizontal concepts of 'distribution', 'spread', 'trajectories', 'networks' and 'flows', in the way that scale is value-loaded, power-invested, ordered and stratified. The link between lower and higher scale-levels is indexicality. A momentary linguistic exchange is uniquely situated in its specific context yet we could understand it because it points to those things at a higher scale-level such as shared patterns of understanding, frames, norms, traditions. The vertical image of scale does not invalidate horizontally distributed space; rather, it offers a complement with a vertical dimension of constructing space.

So far, we have discussed the notion of scale as a spatial metaphor. Let us now turn to the temporal aspect of this notion. As Wallerstein put it, 'time and space are irremediably locked together and constitute a single dimension, which I shall call TimeSpace' (Wallerstein, 1998: 1). A communicative action, or every social action, occurs both in time and in space, and often in multiple space and time frames, such as the five categories of TimeSpace that Wallerstein distinguishes: episodic geopolitical TimeSpace, cyclico-ideological TimeSpace, structural TimeSpace, eternal TimeSpace and transformational TimeSpace (see Wallerstein, 1988, 1991, 1998, for detailed definitions of the terms). By episodic geopolitical TimeSpace, Wallerstein refers to those categories revolving around immediate history, not necessarily current history, but short-term events that derive their meanings from the immediate context in which they occur. 'The Hong Kong handover in 1997' for instance is episodic geopolitical TimeSpace. By cyclico-ideological TimeSpace, Wallerstein means categories by which we make sense of immediate history, as when we account for 'the Hong Kong handover in 1997' by long-standing capitalism–communism differences in the region, or by the United Kingdom's liquidation of British colonialism, or by other definitions of the situation that involve a longer time span. By structural TimeSpace, Wallerstein means categories of long-term phenomena such as the 'rise of Asian Tigers' in the light of the structural explanations of the modern world-system and in the light of the historical and political system in which we live. By eternal TimeSpace, Wallerstein means categories that are of timelessness and spacelessness, or of the irrelevance of time and space. And finally, by transformational TimeSpace, Wallerstein means exactly the opposite, the specialness of the occurrence, its transformational effects on everything subsequent to it. For instance, we can cite the year and place of the 'industrial revolution', more or less, but what matters is the far-reaching transformation that we believe has occurred. Yet, although the particular time and place do not seem to matter, transformational TimeSpace occurs at the only time and space at which it could have occurred (Wallerstein, 1998).

Each category defines TimeSpace at a different level, and a social event often attributes different meanings when positioned in different levels of TimeSpace categories. Scale thus offers not only a vertical metaphor of space, but also a stratified spatiotemporal image of social phenomena. In social interaction, a move from a lower scale of TimeSpace to a higher scale, say, from locally situated to translocal, from momentary to historical, often invokes a move across stratified positions in social order. Consequently, scale needs to be considered as a concept that connects space and time in a fundamental way.

Scale is also a key concept in Wallerstein's World-Systems Analysis, which describes the world as a system of structurally unequal parts organised as 'centres' (high level of capital accumulation, service economy, production of finished goods), 'semi-peripheries' and 'peripheries' (low level of capital accumulation, production of basic resources, dependent on the centres) (Wallerstein, 1983, 2000, 2001). In the domain of sociolinguistics, the centre–periphery model can be expressed, for example, through 'central accents' such as British English and American English, and 'peripheral accents' such as Indian or Nigerian English (Blommaert et al., 2005a). Central accents project central identities, and peripheral accents project peripheral identities. People consume enormous time and energy to acquire English with a British or American accent, but very few attempt to acquire an Indian or Nigerian accent (Blommaert, 2009a). Similar processes of linguistic scaling can be observed in Chinese: Putonghua being a 'central accent', the medium of instruction in schools and an accent that affords mobility across spaces, whereas regional accents are primarily used at home and in informal occasions. In all of these instances, we observe how particular varieties not only indicate regional origin but also produce indexical meanings of layered, stratified space – of centres and peripheries – and hence of identities that 'belong' to such spaces.

These scaling processes are valid at a world level, within a state (e.g. urban vs. rural regions), within a city (e.g. business centres vs. disadvantaged areas) and among neighbourhoods. Spaces are positioned against one another unequally. Some spaces are prestigious, while others project stigma. A move from rural to urban areas in the Chinese context, for instance, is a shift from the periphery to the centre, and central spaces may be difficult and costly to enter. The idea of what is central and what is peripheral in European or Northern American contexts may be reversed from those in the Chinese context, that is, people who can afford it tend to move from cities to the countryside, but the essence of the scaling processes remain the same. In the Chinese context as well as in the European or Northern American context, we observe that such movements take place across time and spaces and across scales of social structure (Blommaert et al., 2005a). The concepts of spatial analysis and scaling processes play key roles in understanding how migrants organise their linguistic repertoires, connect and interact with one another and with others in urban communities, and the phenomenal rural–urban migration in China offers an enormously rich research potential of understanding such movements across spaces and scales, in real terms as well as symbolically. I continue with one more concept – monoglot ideology – before presenting and analysing the data of my fieldwork.

Monoglot ideologies

A monoglot ideology, or 'a culture of monoglot Standard', as Silverstein (1996: 286, 1998) calls it, is characterised by the hegemonic domination of a 'standard language' in a language community. I give a fuller account of the concepts of language community and speech community in Chapter 4. Language community according to Silverstein (1998) refers to people who possess or display allegiance to a shared denotational code of language known by names, for example, English, Chinese or French. Standardisation of a language is a process through which certain valued linguistic practices, or forms of codes, are explicitly recognised and institutionally supported to be the standard. The realisation of the 'standard language' is often singular, in the way that only one clear set of rules and conventions is allowed to be the standard, and other forms are measured against this standard. In that sense, monoglot ideologies can (seemingly paradoxically) also organise *multilingual* situations – think of Belgium, Singapore or Norway – because each of the 'official' language is captured in a monoglot 'standard' frame. The notion of 'standard' or 'standardised' language has long been in the field of linguistic investigation – Leonard Bloomfield addressed this notion in 1927 and regarded the establishment of standards as a result of the functions of hegemonic institutions, for example, the operation of those who control the channels of exemplary usage of language through writing, printing and reading. Hence, 'dialects' are the languages or language varieties that lack the institutionally enforced writing system, normative grammar and so on. Within this monoglot standard, 'best' users of a language are those who speak the standardised form, and to many speakers of standardised language, as Silverstein (1996: 206) points out, the standardised language seems to be the 'natural', the code of 'superiority', a 'superposed' register, whereas varieties other than the standardised one 'do not quite seem to be "real" language'. The standardised language is often imagined to be 'neutral', or 'accent-less' under the monoglot ideology; it is, note, always evidently accented, and perhaps the most noticeably accented one that indexes a baggage of identities of its user, for example, social class, education level, family background, sometimes age group and geographic origin (Blommaert, 2006a). Producing non-standard language, often seen as 'incorrect' at least in schools or other hegemonic institutions of the State, indexes an inadequate level of intelligence or mental slowness, and bespeaks special, or what Blommaert (2006a) calls 'abnormal' identities, a term borrowed from Foucault's psychiatry studies (Blommaert, 2006a; Foucault, 2003).

The monoglot ideology can be illustrated by 'Standard English' in the United States. Silverstein (1996: 286) demonstrates the naturalisation and commoditisation of Standard English in American society. He argues that Standard English has become the 'unifying emblem' of the nation-state, and possession-of-Standard is often turned into an asset that can add to a person's overall value or worth. Furthermore, possession-of-Standard is even seen as a measure of freedom and equality – to free people from 'unwanted' accents and to give them direct and equal access to the 'truth' such as in elections – an idea that has already existed at the time of French Revolution. In many of Silverstein's collected newspaper and magazine articles, regional accents are presented in a seemingly amusing way. However, as Silverstein points out, the popular presentation of an accent or a dialect, especially phonologically, underscores the defects of the accent or dialect, and disqualifies it in relation to Standard English. Similar cases can be found in the first example of this chapter where the Sichuan child is laughed at when introducing herself, as well as in the next chapter where a school pupil suggests that his fellow student can give an example of 'funny' accents.

The monoglot ideology is also studied in Dutch immersion classes for immigrant pupils in three inner city primary schools in the Flemish part of Belgium (Blommaert et al., 2006). In their case study, Blommaert and colleagues observe that the Dutch-speaking teachers establish an ideological link between literacy (often in spelling) and learning, and regard literacy as the prerequisite for any efficient learning. The literacy competence that the teachers value is the specific 'standard Dutch-language literacy in the Latin alphabet', and other forms of reading and writing skills that the pupils have acquired in, for example, Arabic, Cyrillic or English, are treated as low value and in some cases as 'value-less'. 'Grassroots literacy' and basic writing skills developed in linguistic contexts other than standard Dutch are disqualified and denied of the adequate literacy competence, although the pupils effectively map graphemes onto phonemes through their non-Dutch literacy skills. Such skills, under the monoglot ideology that emphasises the standard Dutch language as the only valued linguistic resource, are misrecognised (Bourdieu, 1990; Spotti, 2007). Misrecognition is a power tactic that forces the inferior party to adjust and adapt to the rules of the superior one. The superior, in turn, has no obligation to reciprocate this accommodating move. The immigrant pupils are in effect declared and treated to be 'language-less' and illiterate on the basis that they do not possess the specific literacy skills in the standard Dutch writing system in the 'homogeneous space of a monoglot linguistic community' (Blommaert et al., 2006: 53).

A related notion, 'monolingual habitus', is theorised by Gogolin (1998) in the German and Dutch school contexts. Inspired by Bourdieu's concept of habitus (Bourdieu, 1984, 1987, 1991), Gogolin proposes that monolingual habitus 'is the basic and deep-seated obsession that monolingualism in a society, and particularly in schools, is the one and only, overall, forever and always valid normality' (Gogolin, 1998: 159). Similar to the notion of monoglot ideology, 'monolingual habitus' also addresses the fundamental connections between the establishment of one national language and the disqualification of societal multilingual recourses. The two concepts differ considerably too; remarkably, 'monolingual habitus' is theorised from the perspective of the individual, referring to the monolingualism socialised into the individual, whereas 'monoglot ideology' is positioned on a societal level, emphasising societal plurilingualism, a culture of monoglot Standard, and the hegemonic dominance of Standard English (Silverstein, 1996: 284). The two notions, as I can tell, are the two sides of one coin, and can be applied together fruitfully in identity discourse analysis.

So far, we have looked at three notions: space, scale and monoglot ideology, all of which are important for the reader to engage with the data presentation and analysis in the next section. Moreover, the three theoretical concepts also function as useful analytical tools for studying identity construction on the metapragmatic scale in Chapter 4 as well as the institutional and public scale in Chapter 5.

Space, Accent and Identity Construction

Putonghua and monoglot ideologies

Monoglot ideologies often overlay the societal linguistic diversity that characterises every real social interaction. In China, public discourses on homogeneity of monoglot ideologies often revolve around the unquestioned status of Putonghua, despite the mass population movements that give rise to increasingly intense linguistic exchanges among various social and cultural communities. In order to understand the dominance of Putonghua in the making of migrant identities on the linguistic and communicative scale of everyday interaction, let us examine a newspaper clipping taken from *Ningbo Ri Bao* (*Ningbo Daily*), the official newspaper of the Ningbo city. Ningbo is an emerging industrial and commercial centre in Zhejiang province of the Yangtze River Delta Region in the eastern coastal part of the country. As I described in Chapter 2, the booming manufacturing and trading industries of this region attract millions of migrant workers from rural areas. This story is published as a stand-alone piece in the section of 'readers' stories' of their own life in Ningbo. It is narrated by a primary school student who comes from Sichuan province in the western inland region with her parents and attends a local Ningbo public school.

Example 3.1: '... one day I would speak good Putonghua'

Putonghua makes me a member of this city.

Last summer I arrived in this city with my parents from Sichuan. I was curious about and excited by everything I saw in the streets: skyscrapers, broad streets, and flashing colourful lights in the night. But I felt that all of these were strange and far away from my life, because I was an outsider of this city, a person from elsewhere, a child of migrant workers.

After many twists and turns, my dad found a local school for me. On the first day of the semester, my dad and I came to my new school. 'Wow!' the school was spacious and beautiful in my eyes. My teacher, Miss Zhang, was a pretty young lady who spoke perfect Putonghua. Her Putonghua sounded very nice! She asked me to introduce myself in front of the class, but I couldn't – I couldn't speak Putonghua, how could I introduce myself? Miss Zhang was very kind and asked me to do so in my own dialect. I said 'good morning, I am a child from Sichuan ...' {with marked Sichuan dialect, i.e. 俺是来自四川的娃子 *an shi laizi Sichuan de wazi*, rather than Putonghua 我是来自四川的孩子 *wo shi laizi Sichuan de haizi*}[2] then was interrupted by a loud laughter from the class. I was so embarrassed that I just wanted to run away from the class. You know, I used to be a top student in the school of my hometown; how could I be laughed at like this! Miss Zhang helped me again 'what she used is standard Sichuan dialect'.

After the class, Miss Zhang found me and told me that I should learn Putonghua otherwise I would encounter many difficulties in my life ... Having her kind words in mind I was determined to study hard so that one day I would speak good Putonghua ... Now I have finally got rid of my language barrier and become part of the city. (*Ningbo Daily*, 31.10.06, Issue 11407: 6)[3]

Analysis and interpretation

The story describes a child's migration experience: She travels from Sichuan province to Ningbo city of Zhejiang province, that is, from the periphery to a regional centre. It is not clear as to whether she is from the rural areas of Sichuan or not, but western inland regions, including Sichuan, are generally poorer and economically less developed than eastern coastal regions. The Sichuan accent is therefore an accent of the periphery – a marginal accent. And this marginal accent enters a space in which a 'central' accent dominates, that is, Putonghua. There, it triggers laughter and shame. What is probably a marker of comfortable in-group identity in Sichuan has been downscaled as a marker of rural, peripheral and stigmatised identity in Zhejiang.

The accent is also one of the markers of the city's boundaries. The migrant child is noticeably attracted by the new space, but does not identify herself as a member of the city. Here she encounters accent as the most salient marker of space boundaries – Ningbo is defined by the difference in linguistic variety – as well as a label of her migrant identity. Almost immediately after entering the school she notices that the teacher speaks 'perfect' Putonghua; then she feels incapable of introducing herself because of not speaking the language. The order of indexicality in which the child has entered has become clear now, and the child is 'language-less' (cf. Blommaert *et al.*, 2005a). Her Sichuan accent clearly projects stigma when she introduces herself and she is embarrassed by her peer students' laughter. One trusts that the children do not laugh at her deliberately out of an unfriendly intention. They probably sincerely find the Sichuan accent amusing and hence react without any disguise of their feelings. The local children's spontaneous reaction to her accent, however, precisely points to a social reality that linguistic forms are organised unequally in this particular space, and the Sichuan child's accent is neither usual nor high-ranked in this space: it is an 'abnormal' accent, bespeaking an 'abnormal' identity. This echoes what Silverstein (1996) observes, that the evaluation of an accent as 'amusing' or 'funny' is an ideological utterance highlighting the 'defects' of the accent and measuring it against the standard form of the language.

The teacher suggests that the Sichuan child learns Putonghua in order to integrate with the local urban communities and to have a better chance in life. Notice that differently from Beijing, Ningbo has its local dialects that belong to the Wu dialects, whereas the Sichuan dialects are varieties of Mandarin and is much closer to Putonghua than the Wu dialects phonetically. The teacher does not require the migrant child to learn local Ningbo accent, but Putonghua, for the purposes of social integration. This is what Gogolin (1998: 159) calls the 'monolingual orientation' of teachers' professional habitus, which means that 'it is part of the teachers' profession to traditionalize monolingualism in the official national language'. Gogolin observes this phenomenon in the German context, and compares it with a Dutch classroom observation which describes a Dutch teacher who, although acted out of the best intention, organised her classroom as a result of her monolingual habitus (Kroon, 1986; cited in Gogolin, 1998; Kroon & Vallen, 1991). Here in the Sichuan pupil's case, the monolingual habitus is internalised into the child through the teacher's professional practice. Although the teacher says 'what she used is standard Sichuan dialect' when the migrant child is laughed at by her local peer students, which indicates that the teacher sees acquiring Putonghua as an expansion of the child's linguistic repertoire rather than a substitution of the child's home dialect, the connection she makes between knowledge of Putonghua and opportunities in life ('Miss Zhao told me that I should learn Putonghua otherwise I would encounter many difficulties in my life') is a matter of scale: Putonghua is the language of the government and for public life. It considerably enhances the social mobility across scales, from private to public and from low to high in society, of those who speak it, whereas it functions as a barrier for those who do not speak it. Putonghua as the standard language practically pushes back the 'territories' of local dialects, especially in the contexts of population movements and globalisation.

To summarise, we see three varieties of the Chinese language in action, a fact that questions the language ideology of Chinese being linguistically homogenous. The text describes the child's migration trajectory, from Sichuan to Ningbo, as well as the trajectory of the making of identities. At the beginning of the text, she labels herself as 'an outsider of this city, a person from elsewhere, a child of migrant workers' and explicitly categorises herself as a migrant child; this identity is reinforced by her experience of being laughed at for her accent by her local counterparts at school. Her teacher later talks to the child and asks her to learn Putonghua for her integration into the local society; as Silverstein (1996) points out, the teacher's function reproduces the hegemonic domination of the standard language over the societal linguistic diversity. At the end of the text, the child claims that 'I have finally got rid of my language barrier and become part of the city.' Having adapted successfully to the superior variety, she achieves, or is in the process of achieving, a new identity, the identity of being a local child.

Being silenced by accent

Putonghua often incapacitates those who have limited competence in the standardised variety, diminishes mobility and therefore projects stigmatised identities. Rather than an opportunity, it functions as a constraint for those who do not speak it. The effect is 'misrecognition' in the sense of Bourdieu (1990): despite the intrinsic value of people's symbolic resources, their value is not recognised in particular social contexts, and speakers are left without resources. A monoglot ideology such as the one described in section 'Putonghua and monoglot ideologies' can function, thus, as a silencing instrument that misrecognises the resources that some people possess.

The example that follows (Example 3.2) is drawn from fieldwork observations in a public swimming pool in Liu Zhuang Street,[4] a busy street on the fringe of Beijing. This is a newly developed urban area, highly mixed with local Beijing residents and migrant workers. The northern part of the street is dominated by the local middle class, whereas the southern part is a migrant community (see also section 'Navigating accents and space' below). The swimming pool is run for the local residents, but because of the admission fee, it clearly targets the middle-class consumers living in the northern part of the street, whereas it excludes the migrant community down south of the street. The cleaners of the swimming pool, note, are migrant workers.

Example 3.2: '... none of the listeners understood ...'

> While several young customers stood beside the pool chatting, a middle-aged female cleaner approached them and spoke to them while pointing agitatedly towards the floor. Because of her marked accent, none of the listeners understood what she had to say. From the tone, pitch, and emphases in her speech, it was clear that she complained about something the customers did. The listeners looked at each other puzzled, perhaps annoyed and offended, and then pretended not to hear anything (the loud music could be an excuse) and kept silent. After the cleaner had given up and left, the customers asked one another what the cleaner was talking about. After having established that no one had understood her, they giggled and changed the topic. (Fieldnotes, 2006-10-07)

Analysis and interpretation

The cleaner is a fully competent speaker of her own dialect, and is most probably able to communicate in Putonghua at least on a basic level, because otherwise she would have little chance to be employed in the space – an urban community in Beijing. The space actively values local Beijing accent and standardised Putonghua, whereas it disqualifies the cleaner's accent as valueless. This example echoes and expands what we saw in section 'Putonghua and monoglot ideologies', and in both cases, people with marked regional accents are positioned in spaces that rank their accents low through a scaling process: their language varieties only have limited, local validity; once it is 'exported' to middle-class, urban and central environments it loses function and value, it becomes misrecognised, in the sense that the customers do not understand what the cleaner wishes to address, but choose not to use any communicative technique to find out the meaning, and therefore the interaction terminates – or strictly speaking, little interaction takes place in the encounter. The termination of communication from the listeners' side may result from the difficulty of understanding the speaker, but this explanation is too superficial to address the listeners' silence and ignorance. A more plausible explanation would be that the cleaner's accent, her inability of speaking in the valued variety of the space, perhaps together with her appearance, project her identity as a migrant worker whose speech is not so important that the listeners have to find out the meaning in the local interactive occasion (or the lack of such interaction). Large patterns of social structure – migration and the social positions it produces – seem to collapse here in patterns of interaction. Misunderstanding here is not a matter of just difference, but of difference within a system of inequality. The monoglot ideology described earlier appears to have produced a monolingual habitus (Gogolin, 1998) among people that effectively makes the migrant worker's speech senseless and meaningless.

Navigating accents and space

In the face of such obstacles as discussed in sections 'Putonghua and monoglot ideologies' and 'Being silenced by accent', migrants have to navigate in order to make themselves understood as subjects. Often, such work involves a creative deployment of a wide range of varieties and discursive tactics. The interaction discussed in the following also took place in the same neighbourhood, Liu Zhuang Street. Ten years back it was a rural area, but with the rapid urban expansion, it has been transformed into an urban community with many new residential developments that are particularly popular with young people (who mostly move from central Beijing to this peripheral area of the city, because of the reasonable property price and the efficient transportation links). The influx of new inhabitants creates business opportunities for migrants who relocate to Beijing as low-skilled and poorly paid workers. Due to the difference in economic patterns, the migration in Beijing is rather different from that in the eastern coastal regions. In the coastal regions migrant workers are typically employed in the industrial and manufacturing sectors, such as textile and shoe making, whereas in Beijing, they mainly work in the

Scale 1: Interaction 59

service sector, for example, as garbage collectors, cleaners, domestic workers, breakfast sellers.

Beijing attracts millions of migrants. This street, Liu Zhuang Street, has probably an even higher concentration of migrant workers than central Beijing, because of its proximity to migrant communities' areas: south of the street, big and brand-new buildings gradually give ways to small, shabby houses, with a more rural look and lower hygiene standards in term of facilities such as the lack of running water. The broad clean street turns into a narrow one covered with dust. In that part of the street, I see no more smartly dressed young people rushing to the tube station; instead, I see old people dragging their legs and moving slowly and women washing clothes or feeding children. This is a mixed space filled with both rich and poor. Liu Zhuang Street is a ready example of the centre–periphery model: the northern part (the part with many new developments and near to the tube station) is the centre, and the southern part (migrant area) is the periphery, while the street itself is the periphery in relation to central Beijing.

In what follows I present and analyse a transcript of an audio-taped conversation (Example 3.3) between a migrant worker and me, the researcher, to illustrate how space shapes the way people connect and interact with one another and how spaces are ordered and organised in relation to one another through a centre–periphery model. We have this conversation in Beijing, and I (a native of Beijing) thus represent the 'centre', while the migrant represents the 'periphery'. In the transcript, the migrant whom I shall call Xiao Xu (XX), sells breakfast (*baozi*, steamed dumplings) outside one of the newly developed property complexes in Liu Zhuang Street. I have been a regular customer since Xiao Xu started the breakfast business two months before the recording. In Appendix 2, a transcript is given in *Pinyin*, the official spelling system of Mainland China since 1958. Here, I provide the English translation.

Example 3.3: The street vendor

{traffic noise, people talk unintelligibly}

1   XX: *which ones* (of the steamed dumplings) would you like? {weak and slow voice, noticeably trying to pronounce in local Beijing accent}
    JD: what kinds do you offer?
    XX: here we have ...
5   ... {conversations about the kinds of steamed dumplings he offers}
    JD: you are doing a good business: so many people get their breakfast from you.
    XX: {laughing voice} *only* good in the morning; no one comes in the afternoon {still making efforts to speak in Beijing accent}.
    JD: the morning business is good enough. Have you put the shrimp one in?

```
10  XX:  {nod with smile} that's good – we brought shrimps from hometown.
    JD:  seriously?! Where is it?
    XX:  {proud, smile} they are shrimps from the Yangtze river ... good shrimps
         {noticeably higher and faster, with clearer accent}
         ... {conversations about how they brought the shrimps from their hometown}
15  JD:  you speak good Putonghua, did you learn that from school {smile}?
    XX:  *just so-so*. Some (customers) couldn't figure out what I said {end with laughing
         voice, indicating this is a humble response}
    JD:  I found your Putonghua is really good, I have no problem understand you.
    XX:  well, we learnt Putonghua in school. I studied up to high school {switches from
20       noticeable southern accent to near-Putonghua}
         *are you* a Beijing person?
         {smile, and switch to certain characteristics of Beijing accent}
    JD:  yeah, I am from here.
    XX:  *from here* {low voice, Beijing accent}
25  JD:  did you all use Putonghua in school?
    XX:  we learnt (Putonghua) but also talked in our own dialect.
    JD:  then how comes your Putonghua is so good {smile}?
    XX:  I ... I was here before {switch to Beijing accent, higher, long, jolly voice, indicating
         he was pleased by my comment on his Putonghua, and was proud that
30       he was not a stranger to the city of Beijing}
    JD:  Do you understand what people speak here in Beijing?
    XX:  usually I can, when people talk in their dialects, I can't
         {switches back to Putonghua}.
    JD:  = sure. I can't if they use dialects.
35  XX:  = they use dialects when order steamed dumplings, for a few minutes I don't
         know what they are telling me {end with laughing voice, amused}
    JD:  that's right; also there is very mixed, you can find people from everywhere,
         and many dialects ... .
```

(Fieldwork recording, 2006-10-23-V017)

Analysis and interpretation

Let us take a close look at what happens in the transcript. The most noticeable thing here is the shift of accents in Xiao Xu's discourse, and the shifts appear to be thematic and systematic. First, Xiao Xu greets his customer and attempts to talk with a Beijing accent in the beginning of the conversation from lines 1 to 11 – notice that he uses toneless [mə] that is rare in southern dialects but common in Beijing accent. This can be seen as a commercial talk in which a seller uses business techniques to narrow the gap between him and his customers; at this stage, Xiao Xu does not know whether this customer is a local Beijing person or not. It would make more sense if he used Putonghua; he decides to greet his customers with an attempt to adopt the local accent. Here he speaks in a space – a commercial space of an urban street in Beijing that is presumably filled with local people. This space is peripheral in relation to central Beijing, but central in relation to his hometown. The speaker's relations to space thus actively shape his choice of linguistic forms – the accent he perceives as Beijing accent. Also note that here (in contrast to other parts of the conversation) he uses a low and slow voice, probably signalling the effort he invests in producing this 'central' accent.

The second turn appears when Xiao Xu talks about the shrimps he brought from home in line 12. His voice is higher and faster in this part, along with the shift from his perceived Beijing accent to a more southern accent when the topic of the conversations drifts to his hometown, in which a lexical difference is most obvious: eat/taste is [ch'ri^1] in Putonghua or Beijing accent but [k'e^1] in Xiao Xu's southern accent. This shift of style (in the sense of Blommaert, 2005a: 231 and Rampton, 1999: 423) echoes the observation in the first turn: low and slow voice in the perceived Beijing accent, whereas high and faster voice in his provincial accent. The shift of accents occurs simultaneously with the style shift when the conversations travel across spaces: from Beijing to his hometown in southern China. The shift of accents introduces one more space into the conversations: a far away place where Xiao Xu comes from. The spaces are ordered and organised through a scaling process: Beijing the centre and his hometown, a peripheral place in relation to Beijing; he conducts business in the centre, and uses some of the materials from the periphery.

The third shift occurs in a talk about Xiao Xu's Putonghua in line 19. In this part, I direct the conversation in such a way that Xiao Xu has to talk about how he talks, and how he perceives others talk in this particular space. He reflects that his Putonghua is average, but his laughing voice indicates that he is rather proud of his repertoire and skills in Putonghua. This utterance can be interpreted as a response to my positive comments on his language in line 18 'I found your Putonghua is really good. I have no problem understand you.' This is one of the occasions that the ethnographer should reflect adequately on her influence on the ethnographees and take these reflections on board in data analysis. In line 19, Xiao Xu points out that he has a high school education background. Such a background may give him the access to prestige varieties of Chinese, a semiotic resource from which indexical meanings and values can be derived. As argued above, semiotic resources are layered and stratified; in Xiao Xu's hometown, high school education can be a high-scale resource, and access to such a resource has enabled and enhanced his social mobility. Acquiring Putonghua from his education also facilitates his move across spaces: it is a linguistic resource that affords mobility. However, recall that resources in different spaces are not readily exchangeable, because spaces are positioned in relation to one another unequally, organised through scaling processes. Xiao Xu's movement across spaces is also a movement across scales of social structures. In this fragment of linguistic exchange, Xiao Xu noticeably switches from a southern accent to near-Putonghua, when the conversations change from the shrimps to how he perceives his talk. This accent shift is probably due to an attempt of proving his capability in Putonghua, which occurs simultaneously with the spatial change in the conversation.

Xiao Xu raises a question immediately afterwards, and says: '*are you* a local Beijing person' in line 21, reverting the question–answer pattern, which is established during the conversations. Notice that 'are you' is much weaker and quicker than the rest of the sentence, which is, in one sense quite close to Beijing accent by merging 'are' into 'you' so that the two syllables almost sound like one, but in another sense, making this question less threatening by weakening 'are you'. In the Beijing accent, it can trigger a negative feeling between the interlocutors if 'are you' is emphasised here, implying a challenge of the researcher's position in judging the migrant's linguistic ability. By weakening 'are you' and merging 'are' with 'you', Xiao Xu mitigates the potentially threatening and challenging intention in the utterance.

Xiao Xu's question is interesting in several senses. First, about space and scale: recall that Putonghua is standardised based on the Beijing Mandarin. This projects the prestige status of Beijing accent linguistically as well as sociohistorically. It coincides with Beijing being one of the centres of the country, if not the centre, in a polycentric and stratified system of symbolic spaces as well as spaces in reality. Therefore, Beijing is a space of higher scale than where Xiao Xu comes from, and the Beijing accent, on which Putonghua is standardised, marks this space as a non-neutral non-egalitarian place. The access of the rare resource, that is, high school education, and hence the acquisition of the standard language variety buys Xiao Xu a ticket in the move across space and scales into Beijing.[5]

Second, and more interestingly, Xiao Xu's question displays a performative process of identity construction on a linguistic and communicative level. As discussed in Chapter 1, identities are achieved as well as ascribed, that is, one's self-constructed and claimed identities (the so-called 'achieved' or 'inhabited' identities) have to be recognised by others – ascribed or attributed identities – so as to be established in social reality (Blommaert, 2005a, 2006a, 2006b; Hinnenkamp, 1991; see also Butler, 1990 and Goffman, 1981). Here the conversations prior to the question 'are you a Beijing person' trigger the dialogical practice of establishing individual identities. Before Xiao Xu's question, the conversations are about his hometown, his Putonghua and his education background. I, being a local person and thus representing the 'centre', assume a role of judging Xiao Xu's accent, although in a friendly and encouraging way, enacting the indexical meaning on wider and bigger sociolinguistic issues such as the place of origin, education level and social categorisation. Xiao Xu's question leads the conversations into an explicit social interaction in which identities are claimed and ratified in a performative and mutual process.

Xiao Xu's individual identity is not a singular and stable category but a repertoire of multiple identities that are organised unequally in relation to the access of the identity building resources: It is a spectrum of possible categories that have been produced through access to the semiotic resources that construct identities and carry layered value. As the semiotic resources are stratified, so are the identities. Identity in one space may not be readily converted into its counterpart in another space: One may be an important person in his village, but may become nobody in a big city. The access to high school education projects a prestige identity in Xiao Xu's hometown, but does not project a similar identity in Beijing, the central space in the centre–periphery model.

There are several layers of Xiao Xu's multi-identities displayed in the conversation: When he speaks about the shrimps from his hometown, he switches to a marked provincial accent that indexes his identity of coming from that particular place; him being of provincial and I being central. During his talk about his Putonghua, he shifts to a near-Putonghua accent that enacts his identity of high social mobility and hence an elite identity. But this identity is fluid and shifting: as mentioned above, identity does not travel easily across spaces, and therefore he is in a process of seeking ratification of his identity in a new and up-scale space.

In line 24 he repeats my answer 'from here' in a low voice, trying to reproduce the utterances in the same way that I do, with an [r] attached to 'here' (*zhe* + *er* in Chinese) to make it a marked Beijing accent. This echoes his fourth shift of linguistic style in line 28 'I was here before.' Here Xiao Xu switches from a low, weak voice in line 24 to a higher, prolonged and jolly voice, indicating a positive response to my comments on his Putonghua, but also emphasising that he learnt Putonghua partly from the interactions with local people, that this is not his first spatial movement from his hometown, and therefore he is not one of the 'others' when interacting with a local person. 'Othering' is a process of social categorisation of other people. Given the fact that Xiao Xu owns the business, plus his earlier experiences of the city, he may have achieved a new local identity, or at least an identity of burgeoning entrepreneur in Beijing. This is confirmed in the later conversations between him and me about how he set up the business and what he plans to do in the future. This newly achieved identity needs to be recognised through a performative process such as this one in the central space.

The next part is on how Xiao Xu perceives other regional accents and dialects. He indicates that his Putonghua is usually enough to understand people who speak in Putonghua, but not those when they use their respective dialects. Simultaneously he switches back to near-Putonghua and lays emphasis on 'their' in the utterances 'talk in their dialects', to imply that 'they' use dialects, 'I' or 'we' do not. This is an othering process in which he categorises people who use dialect as 'others', but himself and me as 'us'. Later in the conversation (not transcribed here) he speaks about this experience of working in Shanghai, one of the central spaces of the country similar to Beijing and another popular destination for migration in southern China, and comments that local Shanghai people of lower class cannot or are not willing to speak Putonghua, because of inadequate education or low awareness of the importance to speak Putonghua. His comments confirm the observations of the othering process when he says that *others* talk in their dialects whereas *he* and *I* use Putonghua. Here education is again a rare resource, so is Putonghua, and both project prestige identities. The way Xiao Xu organises his accents in interaction with me, his local customer, reflects the centre–periphery model of spaces, from Liu Zhuang Street to central Beijing, from Beijing to Xiao Xu's hometown. And the spaces are ordered in the hierarchical social structure through scaling processes.

So far, we have examined in detail what happens in the fragment of the conversations. To summarise, we can distinguish a series of accent shifts in Xiao Xu's utterances. The shifts start from line 12 and stop in line 31, each time in a mix with a near Beijing accent. The fragments prior and after that part are spoken in a near Beijing accent (lines 1–11) and Putonghua (lines 32–38). These shifts in accent are part of a bigger series of shifts in the conversation: the three units are topical as well, and the topical shifts correlate with the accent shifts. They later also correlate with identity shifts: Xiao Xu speaks differently and *as a different person* in each of the units (Blommaert & Dong, 2009b).

In the first unit, he is a breakfast seller, which is a commercial identity; in the second topical unit he speaks as a migrant who comes from the South and has acquired Putonghua at school; the shift to the topic of the other, more recent, migrants in the area triggers again another role. He now aligns with his interlocutor and appears to define himself as an inhabitant of the local Beijing neighbourhood. The migrant identity has been replaced by a local identity, and he expresses a sense of belonging in and entitlement to a place. He is from an earlier generation of migrants

Table 3.1 Summary of the shifts

Unit	Space	Accent	Identity
Unit 1 (1–11)	Commercial	Putongua, Beijing accent	Breakfast seller
Unit 2 (12–31)	The South and Beijing	Southern accent, Beijing accent	A migrant from the South
Unit 3 (32–38)	Neighbourhood	Putongua	Local resident

and in contrast to newer migrants, he is a local man. Here we observe complexes of linguistic patterns, that is, accents and communicative styles, systematically deployed towards topics and interlocutors, and an equally complex articulation of identities. On the linguistic and communicative scale, a range of identities – from a dumpling seller, to a migrant from the South and a local man – are enacted, performed, claimed, negotiated, challenged, ratified; the identities are rather fluid and situational, ever changing as Xiao Xu takes different positions according to the topics and the spaces of the interaction, and the shifts in positioning articulate different categories of identity. The positioning is what Goffman (1981: 128) called 'footing' – the alignment one takes up to oneself and others in a communicative event – and the shift in footing flags a change in the alignment during the interaction.

Summary

In this chapter I illustrate migrant identity construction at the level of local interaction. To recap briefly, I discuss three analytical notions: space, scale and monoglot language ideology. They were not to be considered as preconceived concepts; rather, they were theorised in sociolinguistics, sociology, linguistic anthropology as well as other related domains and shed new light on the identity building process in linguistic exchanges and communicative events. I present and analyse three examples to illustrate the linguistic processes of identity making on the first scale of the general theoretical framework laid out in Chapter 1 – the linguistic and communicative scale. The first example points to a connection between the acquisition of Putonghua and better opportunities in life, which reflects the monoglot ideology of language. Putonghua enables social mobility of those who speak it, whereas it functions as a barrier for those who do not speak it. This I also observe in the second example, in which the migrant worker's linguistic resources are disqualified as peripheral. In both examples we see that the monoglot ideology produces a monolingual habitus that makes some people's speech meaningless – in the first example the Sichuan child introducing herself to local pupils, and in the second example the cleaner attempting to communicate with middle-class customers.

However, migrant workers are not always silenced by the collective monolingual habitus. I do not intend to suggest, either through the examples of this chapter or through those of the following chapters that migrant workers are always discriminated against because of their accents. They can navigate these obstacles by deploying the different codes and registers tactically in their social encounters. Such cases appear in the third example. Xiao Xu displays complicated linguistic patterns involving characteristics of three language varieties: Beijing accent, Putonghua and an accent of southern China. This example illustrates the fluidity and flexibility of identities constructed on the linguistic and communicative scale, through Xiao Xu's various identities from a breakfast seller, to a migrant from the South, and then to a local resident, as he deploys a range of linguistic patterns oriented towards the shift of topics. Identities constructed at this scale are shifting and situational. Such identities, however, often point to and are conditioned by those at higher-level scales – the metapragmatic discourse scale, and the public and institutional discourse scale. In the next chapter, I therefore focus on the making of migrant identity on the second scale – metapragmatic discourse scale – and demonstrate how claimed identities are challenged, ratified, negotiated, ascribed through people's explicit evaluative remarks.

Notes

1. An earlier version of this chapter, titled 'Space, Scale and Accents: Constructing Migrant Identity in Beijing', was published in *Multilingua* 28(1), 1–24.
2. The differences in lexicon usage between Putonghua and Sichuan dialect are summarised as follows:

	In writing	*In Pinyin*	*In writing*	*In Pinyin*
Putonghua	我	*wo*	孩子	*haizi*
Sichuan Dialect	俺	*an*	娃子	*wazi*
Meaning in English	I		child	

Scale 1: Interaction

3. The newspaper is available online at: http://www.cnnb.com.cn/gb/node2/newspaper/nbrb/2006/10/node69731/node69749/index.html. Last accessed on 15.7.09; the complete account of the story can also be found in its original form of Chinese characters in Appendix II.
4. Both the street name and the migrant's name are kept anonymous.
5. This is not to say that only those who have high school education are mobile, many do migrate without much schooling; however, it does, together with the acquisition of Putonghua, facilitate the mobility in Xiao Xu's case.

Chapter 4
Scale 2: Metapragmatic Discourses

Introduction

This chapter reports on the study of identity construction on the second scale, the scale of metapragmatic linguistic practice. This scale deals with metapragmatic discourses on migrant people's language and identity. The data in this chapter are all extracted from my fieldwork conducted in a Beijing public primary school between January and August 2007. Schools, and the educational system in general, are among the key institutions that embody dominant social values and reproduce social structure in a seemingly neutral form – a form often perceived as common practice. In Beijing schools, as in other parts of China, an increasing number of migrant pupils from various social and linguistic backgrounds enter into interaction with their local counterparts and with educational practitioners on a daily basis. The microscopic linguistic differences between migrant pupils and local pupils and teachers that occur in such interactions often index metapragmatic factors at a language-ideological level and serve as a ground for the dialogical process of identity construction among pupils.[1]

To explain how migrant identities are negotiated and established on the metapragmatic scale, I deploy the notions of ethnolinguistic identity and speech community (Blommaert, 2005a, 2006b; Gumperz, 1968; Rampton, 1998; Silverstein, 1996, 1998, 2003) as the central analytical tools to examine empirical data from my ethnographic fieldwork in the educational arena. In what follows I first introduce these central notions, and second, I present four examples of migrant identity construction through evaluative metapragmatic remarks of migrant pupils as well as Beijing local pupils and teachers.

Central Concepts: Speech Community and Ethnolinguistic Identity

The notion of speech community has an intellectual history of more than a century. It runs from Herder's assumption about the automatic relations between language and community (i.e. a people, nation, ethnic group), to the De Saussure's collective 'mass of speakers', and Bloomfield's frequency of communication – a behaviourist definition of speech community. The linguistic anthropological approaches have increasingly provided arguments for revising the definition of speech community. In this current of changes, John Gumperz' fieldwork in a North Indian village and a Northern Norwegian town demonstrates that the quality of interaction is as important as the frequency of contact, if not more, in language convergence and differentiation processes. A speech community is defined by Gumperz as 'a field of action where the distribution of linguistic variants is a reflection of social facts' (Gumperz, 1968: 383). This definition emphasises multilingualism and linguistic repertoires rather than presumed uniformity (Gumperz, 2003; Gumperz & Hymes, 1972).

The rise of language ideology as a separate field of enquiry in linguistic anthropology facilitates the understanding of the concept of speech community by drawing in key insights from the social-scientific study of ideology (cf. Kroskrity, 2000). In a language ideology approach, Michael Silverstein (1998) distinguishes speech communities from language communities, arguing that language communities are ideological constructs; they entail people's allegiance to a shared denotational code of language known by names (e.g. English, French and Chinese). In contrast, speech communities are practical constructs, comprised of speakers that display joint orientations towards 'presupposable regularities' and such sharedness of indexical values can result in the construction of identities and communities (Silverstein, 1998; see also Blommaert, 2006b). Therefore, a language community is a specific kind of speech community, in which people display a shared orientation towards the presupposition of normative usage resulting in ethnolinguistic identity associated with the denotational code, for example, 'I am a native speaker of Chinese,' or 'I speak Mandarin.'

Ethnolinguistic identities such as 'I am a native speaker of Chinese' are often taken for granted, but when we look into the so-called 'Chinese language' closely, things become more complex on the ground. As we have seen in Chapter 2, many languages and dialects are spoken in this part of the world; the linguistic classification of languages and dialects is, however, very problematic, as it notably overlooks the intra-linguistic differences within a language or a dialect. One may find it difficult to count the varieties within the *Min* dialects, for example. Once a *Min* speaker reflects that the local vernacular varies so greatly that she cannot understand people of another village 10 miles away from her own (Fieldnotes, 2006-03). In the actual practice of social life, languages and dialects are often linked with particular places, such as *Henan* dialects – the dialects spoken in the Henan province. This categorisation is also problematic. An informant whose place of origin is the Henan province points out to me that his own accent is closer to that of his Anhui classmate than the Henan ones, because his home village is near to the borders of Anhui province (Fieldnotes, 2008-04-11). These examples show that 'language community' is an ideological construct based on *imagined* linguistic boundaries, and the practical alignment in actual communicative activities has little to do with language names. The identities constructed through such communicative activities are not as homogeneous and static as ethnolinguistic identities suggest: the Henan informant is a speaker of Henan dialects by the definition of ethnolinguistic identity, and he believes that he is a native speaker of Henan dialects, but the actual identities articulated by his linguistic practice are multiple – talking in Henan dialects with those who are from the same province project a regional identity; using his particular variety of 'Henan' dialect with his friend, the Anhui classmate, signals a shift in orientation towards shared indexicalities of that specific locality; moreover, the Henan informant tells me the story in Putonghua that enacts identity aspects – being well educated and of high social mobility. I use the notions of 'speech community' and 'ethnolinguistic identity' in the next section, because these notions allow us to look beyond the established language names and categories such as 'language' and 'dialect' into the actual language usage and the identities they index (Dong & Blommaert, 2009; cf. Hymes, 1996).

Language Ideology, Speech Community and Identity

The school

The school under study is located in a narrow and old lane of central Beijing. The area used to be inhabited by local people, but gradually many of them have moved to newly built complexes on the outskirts of Beijing because the old single storey houses in central Beijing area are uncomfortable and inconvenient (usually without such facilities as private bathroom, washroom and running water). The area is now largely occupied by urban low-income households who originally lived here, and migrant families who rent rooms from those who moved out. Migrant families rent rooms or flats in the area often because they do low-skilled jobs in or offer service to the neighbourhood, working as cleaners hired by the neighbourhood committee (*juweihui*), or fruit and vegetable sellers in the nearby markets. The rent may cost less on the outskirts of the city, but the transport costs

Scale 2: Metapragmatic Discourses 71

are considerable, and many of their jobs require an early starting hour (for the vegetable sellers the day begins at around two in the morning). The children of migrant families who rent rooms or flats in the neighbourhood are admitted into Beili School, which is subsidised and managed by the district educational authority (*qu jiaoyuju*).[2]

As discussed in Chapter 2, migrant children's education is often hindered in cities; the Beili School is, however, an exception which receives financial supports from the local educational authority for admitting migrant pupils who do not possess a local *hukou*. This school therefore offers a rare fieldwork site of observing linguistic interactions between the migrant pupils and their local Beijing counterparts as well as of obtaining the evaluative remarks on migrant pupils' linguistic features and identities from the local teachers and the local pupils. There are around 200 pupils in the school, of which about half are migrant children. They were mostly born and raised in Beijing, although none of them managed to obtain a Beijing *hukou*. I observed that the migrant pupils almost always use Putonghua and sometimes with Beijing local accent in school.

Migrant pupils' metapragmatic discourses on their languages and identities

As discussed above, ethnolinguistic identities are often perceived as 'natural'. This is also observed in China, despite of its linguistic complexity with many languages and language varieties. Such identities function within ideologies of homogeneity and uniformity – monoglot language ideologies that overlay the societal diversity. Often monoglot ideologies, produced and circulated through metapragmatic activities, are dominant in schools, and schools at the same time reproduce such ideologies. In order to understand the construction of migrant identities at the metapragmatic level within monoglot ideologies, let us look at the following data.

Example 4.1: 'We all speak Putonghua'

> The setting was a drawing class; the pupils were asked to draw their friends in groups of three or four. I joined one of the groups and a pupil of that group drew me, but another one commented that what she drew didn't look like me because of the hair style – it was the hair style of countryside girls and mine was not. The girl who drew me was not pleased with this comment, and said 'So what? We are all from the countryside. Aren't you a rural girl too? Don't forget you came from the same place as me.' I felt the debate heating, interrupted them and asked 'is there any difference, countryside and city?' in an attempt to

ease the tension, and the pupil who drew me replied 'isn't it enough that we are all <u>Chinese</u>? See we all speak <u>Putonghua</u>' (with a clear emphasis on the words 'Chinese' and 'Putonghua'). Then we changed the topic and commented on drawings. (Fieldnotes, 2007-06-14)

Analysis and interpretation

The pupil who draws me is one of the migrant pupils, and the other pupil who comments on the hairstyle comes from the same province. They are both about 10 years old. It is amazing to see a 10-year-old being offended by identity comments and articulating a clear discourse on language and identities. There are several layers of identities displayed in the account. First, the girl who comments on the drawing distinguishes me from the rural population and ascribes me an urban identity. Here the ways people dress, move and talk collectively serve as identity markers. The comment is made in a friendly and innocent way, but it triggers the dialogical practice of establishing group and individual identities. The pupil who draws me reacts with a series of provocative questions without expecting any answer. This can be considered as the second layer of the identity discourse: her questions points to an awareness of the rural–urban divide – that the pupil who draws as well as the pupil who comments are from a rural area that ranks low in relation to Beijing, whereas I, the fieldworker, am someone from 'here'. From a talk with their teacher at the beginning of my fieldwork, I learn that the school and teachers try to create an egalitarian atmosphere in which there is no difference between the migrant and the local, to protect the migrant children from being alienated or discriminated against. Consequently, the teacher concludes that the students have no knowledge on who are urban and who are not. It is well intended to neutralise the rural–urban divide, but such a divide is a social construct and school (pupils and teachers alike) by no means functions in a social vacuum. From this episode, it is clear that the pupils as young as 10 years old have a good understanding of their identity categorisations to be first of rural origins and second, rural people immigrated to cities. Both identities (i.e. the identities of being of rural origin and migrant identities) are stigmatised and stigmatising, in the sense of Goffman (1974b). Stigma is an undesirable difference people bear, when measured against the 'normal' (see a more detailed account of this notion in Chapter 5).

The pupil's final comment is particularly informative. Recall what she says 'isn't it enough that we are all <u>Chinese</u>? See we all speak <u>Putonghua</u>'. Immediately prior to this utterance, I interrupt the two pupils and ask whether there is any difference between countryside and city, and the tone of this question implies a negative answer – no difference between the two. This interruption is intended to ease the tension, as noted in the field diary, but it makes the rural–urban divide explicit in this interactional event and unexpectedly triggers the final comment. Although she is aware of her (and the other pupil's) special identities, she 'jumps' the scale and blurs the rural and urban identities by overlaying them with a national identity – being Chinese people. The scale-jumping movement from a rural to a national identity is made through the language – Putonghua, what Hymes (1968: 25) calls a 'one language-one culture' assumption which argues that 'the ethnographic world can be divided into "ethnolinguistic" units, each associating a language with a culture'. Here Putonghua is assumed to be the medium of 'the Chinese culture' which is seen as a homogeneous whole, and through this language people acquire another layer of identity – the ethnolinguistic identity. In this episode, claiming the ethnolinguistic identity of being Chinese can be seen as a tactic of avoiding the stigmatised migrant identities.

It is clear that the pupil who draws me is aware of her rural origin and most probably also aware of the negative image such an identity projects. However, she overlays this migrant identity with a national identity and this utterance points to a recognisable ethnolinguistic identity category through the claimed belonging to a homogeneous language community. These two identity categories, migrant identity and ethnolinguistic national identity, are neither contradictory to nor exclusive of each other; rather, they function at different scales: At the scale of rural–urban contrast functions the migrant identity, an identity that is to be discouraged (by the school and the teachers) from mentioning and is to be obscured, if not erased (by the migrant pupil); at the scale of collective membership to a homogeneous community functions the ethnolinguistic identity; through jumping to this scale by using and emphasising the national identity the migrant pupil bypasses the stigmatised 'migrant identity'.

Notice that the obscuring of migrant identity with a national identity is taken for granted by a migrant pupil, rather than a local pupil or a teacher in the social space. Her move towards a homogeneous 'national' identity layer is an ideological move, or an internalisation of the social structure in people (Bourdieu, 1987). In the migrant pupil's identity discourse, the pupil takes on board the migrant identity ('Don't forget you came from the same place as me'), if unwillingly, but she nevertheless makes sense of the world around her, of the social strata she is caught up in, perhaps also of her escape of the 'unwanted' identity, through the scale-jumping phenomenon we observe in her metapragmatic discourse demonstrated in this example.

This migrant identity construction on the level of metapragmatic discourse can be further illustrated by another example of a group interview among migrant pupils during a class break. The group of pupils, also aged 10, are from the same class of the first example.

Example 4.2: 'We all speak dialect at home'

During the break some pupils chatted with me. They were cheerful and loud, raising their voices and competing with each other for my attention. I asked them where they came from, and whether they could show me their dialects; a girl told me that she came from Jiangxi province, and she could speak Jiangxi dialect, but refused to do so in front of me. Why? I asked. 'There is nothing for me to use my dialect' {with a prolonged and emphasised 'nothing' indicating reluctance and shyness}. Laughter from the children. A boy joined in, pointing to another girl and said she could speak Zhejiang dialect. The girl said 'Hmm, no, I can't (speak Zhejiang dialect). I was born in Beijing, of course I speak Putonghua ...' A third girl said 'I am from Henan province. I speak the dialect at home with my mum ...' The boy said 'We are all like that – we all speak dialects at home with our parents.' I begged the children to show me just a little bit of their dialects, so that I could learn. The Jiangxi girl said something in her dialect, laughing. I asked her to repeat it so that I could follow, but she laughed and refused to try it again. Why? 'Because it doesn't sound good.' But why? 'It sounds terrible, it sounds like a foreign language. If I talk to others like this, they would think I talk in a foreign language ...' 'The northeast accent is most funny,' the boy said, 'if you want to learn dialects, teacher, you'd better find Fangfang, because she is good at that.' Fangfang is a local Beijing child, the class representative. By then most of the pupils had left me. (Fieldnotes, 2007-05-30)

Analysis and interpretation

This extract reconstructs conversations between the pupils and me, the class observer. The pupils are very articulate. They surround me and try to talk to me during class break, but the Jiangxi girl becomes unusually shy when I ask about her dialect; she refuses to perform it in front of me at the beginning. Being reluctant for a while, she displays her dialect very briefly, in response to my gentle but persistent request. Jiangxi province is located in central south China, and is one of China's poorest provinces. When asked to repeat it, she is determined not to do so, and declares that the dialect sounds 'terrible', 'like a foreign language'. The Jiangxi pupil's comments on language use indicate that she has a good idea of the differences between her home language and Putonghua, and also that the differences are not neutral. In her evaluative remarks, the dialect is ranked low through a scaling process, although unconsciously, and is labelled with negative features. Her reaction points to a social reality that linguistic forms are organised unequally within monoglot ideologies, and such monoglot ideologies qualify Putonghua as the 'correct' language whereas other dialects as improper and inadequate.

The monoglot ideologies are made clearer in the Zhejiang girl's comment 'I can't (speak Zhejiang dialect). I was born in Beijing and of course I speak Putonghua ...' This utterance shows that Putonghua is unquestionably *the* language and there is no room for dialects in the social space. The assumption in the Zhejiang girl's comments is that she was born and grows up in Beijing; here everyone speaks Putonghua and it is only natural that she speaks Putonghua. The assumed naturalness of Putonghua overlays linguistic diversity in everyday encounters, such as what the street corner example (Example 3.3) demonstrates, and it indexes the homogeneity and uniformity in the social context of Beijing city.

Following the Jiangxi pupil's negative qualification of her dialect as 'terrible' and 'foreign', the boy suggests that I should learn the northeast dialect from Fangfang, a local Beijing pupil, because the northeast dialect is 'most funny' and Fangfang is good at it. This is particularly informative in two ways. First, the northeast dialect is described as 'funny', which seemed not as negative as the Jiangxi pupil's evaluation of her dialect. However, whether being 'funny' or 'terrible', the dialects are abnormalised – being seen as not normal; rarely anyone would suggest Putonghua as 'funny' or 'terrible' – Putonghua is just 'normal'. This utterance echoes Silverstein's (1996) observation that presenting an accent or a dialect in an amusing way highlights the defects of the language variety, and in fact disqualifies it. Second, being migrant children and native speakers of dialects to various degrees, the group of pupils are almost all hesitant in and embarrassed by showing me their home language, but direct me to a Beijing pupil for the knowledge of dialects. I later have a small chat with Fangfang and she indicates that she never really learns any dialect; she occasionally mimics some dialects but she doesn't think that she is particularly talented in that. It is clear that the migrant children's home language, that is, the dialects of their parents, is not something that make the migrant pupils proud. In contrast, Beijing Mandarin is the original form of Putonghua, and the Putonghua spoken by Beijing people is often assumed as a standard. The Beijing pupil, as someone who can speak dialect and who is known as being a non-dialect speaker, is put in the position to give examples of regional dialects, precisely because she is a native speaker of the prestige variety which secures her identity as a Beijing person, and this also gives her the authority of, with some talent in mimicking accents, telling others what a dialect is like.

We see several varieties of Chinese language in action, and this questions the language ideology of Chinese being linguistically homogenous. Moreover, the migrant children's metapragmatic comments on their language use (i.e. home languages, dialects, Putonghua) show us the ways that languages as well as identities are evaluated, negotiated and constructed. The identities studied in the first and the second examples are inhabited identities, that is, identities that are self-constructed and self-performed. The next two examples instantiate how migrant identities are also ascribed by local pupils and teachers.

Local Beijing pupil's metapragmatic discourses and migrant identity construction

Ascribed identity, as opposed to inhabited identity, is another aspect of the identity construction process addressed in this chapter. Identities that are attributed to someone by others are within the domain of ascribed identities. Example 4.3 is a metapragmatic discourse of a local Beijing pupil on how his migrant classmate talks. In his metapragmatic evaluation, the migrant pupil's linguistic features (e.g. accents) are related to identity issues and the social category of 'migrants' is ascribed to the pupil.

Example 4.3: 'She is a migrant and can't get it right'

> Interview with Jun, a local boy, during class break on 12 June 2007. Xing is Jun's migrant classmate.

1	JD:	Do you share a table with Xing?
	Jun:	Yeah.
	JD:	How is her Chinese, her pronunciation?
	Jun:	Pronunciation, <u>very</u> bad.
5	JD:	Is her (pronunciation) unclear?
	Jun:	Yeah, like, we say '<u>cuo</u>', she says '<u>chuo</u>'.
	JD:	Does she have an accent?
	Jun:	She is a <u>migrant</u> child.
	JD:	So (that's why) she is not very clear (in her pronunciation)?
10	Jun:	I am from here.
	JD:	I know you are from here {with a smiling voice}. But do you think that (her accent) influences her Chinese?

Scale 2: Metapragmatic Discourses

Jun: Yeah. <u>People from other places</u> are always unclear.
JD: Do you help her with her pronunciation?
15 Jun: <u>Yeah I do help her</u>, but she just <u>can't make it right</u>! She (is) a <u>migrant</u> and <u>can't</u> get it right.
JD: Do you feel (there is) any difference between her and us?
Jun: (I feel that) they migrants speak differently; very often I <u>can't figure out what she is saying</u>.
20 JD: Difficult to communicate?
Jun: Yeah. Once I was sitting and doing something, she came to me and said, 'XXXXXXX' {unintelligible talk}
JD: {laughing voice} but you couldn't understand…
Jun: I couldn't! She was very *silly* {low voice as if to tell me a secret}.

(Fieldwork recording, 2007-06-12-V049)

Analysis and interpretation

The interview is taken during class break after several weeks of non-participant observation in the class. There are 21 pupils, 12 girls and nine boys, five local and 16 migrants. Most of them are eight years old. The classroom is organised in rows, with two pupils sitting in pairs so that they can work together. There is a blackboard at the front of the classroom and teachers stand between the blackboard and the pupils. Jun is a local boy who sat next to Xing. They have a lot of interaction in and out of class. The section immediately prior to the interview is a Chinese lesson (*yuwenke*) in which the teaching is focused on the pupils' pronunciation of Chinese characters – the teacher writes Chinese characters on the blackboard and chooses pupils to read the characters loudly. The pupils are all eager to get a chance by raising hands and shouting 'teacher, teacher …' or 'ask me, ask me …'. Xing catches the teacher's attention, stand up and read a character loudly but with 'incorrect' pronunciation ('incorrect' in the sense of educational arena). The pupils are disappointed by her performance; almost everyone in the classroom shouts to 'correct' her, and Jun is the loudest. They shout because they have all volunteered to read the character: Xing gets the chance to do so but she does not make good use of the opportunity. Xing is embarrassed and her facial expressions indicate a clear sense of inadequacy.

This episode triggers my interview with Jun, a local Beijing boy speaking with a marked Beijing accent. After a few casual questions, I start asking for his comments on Xing's language. In line 4 he assesses Xing's pronunciation to be '<u>very</u> bad', and emphasised 'very'. The utterance is in a clearly identifiable Beijing accent, and together with the particular emphasis on 'very', it carries connotation that something is more than 'very bad'. Then I push him for more details and he gives an example that what he pronounces as 'cuo' (starting with consonant [ts'], meaning 'wrong'), Xing would pronounce as 'chuo' (starting with consonant [ch'r], meaning 'more'). Many dialects do not distinguish the dental sibilants (*z*, *c*, *s*) from the retroflexes (*zhi*, *ch*, *sh*). As Robert Ramsey demonstrates, the distinction is a mark of standard Putonghua and the mastery of such subtle differences is much admired by people living outside of the capital; they are often unable to pronounce these sounds in the standard way and most do not even try to imitate the 'correct' forms. In practice, people get along without the distinctions (Ramsey, 1987: 43–44).

However, the small linguistic feature indexes big identity issues. Immediately after his description of how Xing talked, Jun points out that Xing 'is a migrant child'. This does not answer my question 'Does she have an accent?' Instead of commenting on her language, Jun sticks an identity label of 'migrant identity' on Xing, linking her accent directly with identity. This direct link between accent and identity is a classic example of indexicality, in which an accent *points to* an identity (cf. Blommaert, 2005a; Coupland, 2007; De Fina *et al.*, 2006; Silverstein, 1998 for indexicality, accent and identity). I keep on asking Jun about Xing's way of talking: 'so that she is not very clear (in pronouncing words)', but once again Jun puts the inquiry on linguistic aspects aside and focuses on identity 'I am from here' in line 10. This comment is interesting in several ways. First, Jun dodges my question for the second time, which indicates that the idea that Xing is a migrant is strong enough to make him ignore the questions of a class observer who is regarded and respected as a second teacher in the classroom.

Second, there are jumps in his answers: in line 8 he said 'She is a migrant child' and in line 10 'I am from here'. What is missing in his comments can be interpreted as 'She is a migrant child' and therefore she speaks with an accent, and 'I am from here' a local Beijing person who speaks the 'right' language and is thus in a position to judge Xing's accent. This interpretation is confirmed by his later comments in lines 13, 15 and 16. In this sense, Jun answers my questions by relating linguistic features with identities again, and the identities are not equal – Jun is a local child and has the access to the prestige resource of the Beijing accent. Xing's identity is ranked lower as the semiotic resources she has access to and deploys are stigmatising. The two identities – migrant identity and local Beijing identity – are organised unequally in relation to access to the identity building resources – a regional dialect and a Beijing accent – and as the semiotic resources are stratified (i.e. the Beijing accent is ranked higher than Xing's dialect), so are the identities.

The utterance 'People from other places³ are always unclear' (line 13) classifies anyone who is not a local Beijing person as 'others' (Rampton, 1999, 2008). In this classification the enormous diversity of the Chinese language is overlaid by the idea that all non-Beijing speakers share a similar feature of being 'always unclear'. Jun generalises his perception of one migrant's language to all immigrants and, rather artificially, distinguishes 'Beijing speakers' and 'non-Beijing speakers' as two language communities, whether or not the latter group share the same indexicalities.

Jun assumes the position to assess Xing's language again in line 15 and comments that it is difficult to 'help' her, and she simply cannot manage the 'right' form, because, note, 'She (is) a migrant and can't get it right' (lines 15 and 16). Jun's language is taken for granted as the 'correct' form of language and as a standard against which Xing's language is measured, disqualified and to be corrected. This utterance again evokes the indexicalities between language and identity – Xing enters a space where 'central' accent dominates, that is, Putonghua or Beijing local accents; her communicative ability is misrecognised, and she has to adjust and adapt to the rules of the dominant ones (i.e. native speakers of the Beijing dialects whose accent indexes a local identity) of the social space. The dominant ones, in contrast, have no obligation to reciprocate this accommodating move.

In line 17 I ask Jun to describe the differences he perceives between his and Xing's language features 'Do you feel (there is) any difference between her and us.' I use 'us' in the question and hence introduce (although unintentionally) the idea of Jun and me the researcher being 'us' (i.e. local Beijing people) and by the same token Xing being one of 'them' (i.e. migrants) as opposed to 'us'. It also triggers Jun's use of 'they' to refer to migrants in line 18. My utterances as an interviewer definitely plays a role in the conversations and this role should be adequately reflected in the analysis. I am also a 'native speaker' of a Beijing dialect, apart from a research, and my accent articulates a local Beijing identity. Despite being a trained ethnographic researcher, I am still caught up in ideologies, even ideologies that I critique. The linguistic and non-linguistic products of these ideological processes appear in the fieldwork, for example, the 'us' in line 17 and the '{laughing voice}' in line 23, both of which is meant to emphasise alignment and to create an unthreatening atmosphere for the eight-year-old. These verbal and non-verbal signs, however, undoubtedly influence the interviewee's comments, and contribute to reproducing the dominant social value and hierarchy. This is a learning process in fieldwork, and what an ethnographer could do is but to document such occasions and to be reflexive on my own role in the research (see Blommaert & Dong [2010] for a fuller discussion on such forms of 'data pollution).

As for the question 'Do you feel (there is) any difference between her and us' in line 17, Jun does not comment on Xing's language but, again, responds in a generalising way – 'they migrants speak differently ... I <u>can't figure out what she is saying</u>' in line 18 and 19. By referring to 'they migrants' he is speaking from the top of the 'pyramid', not on one person's language, but on migrants as a whole who speak differently and with whom Jun finds it difficult to communicate. He shows his frustration on breakdowns of communication between himself and Xing by a loud enunciation '<u>can't figure out what she is saying</u>'. Xing is the one who causes the 'problem'.

In lines 21 and 22, Jun half-jokingly imitates Xing's language by unintelligible talk 'XXXXXXX' in which Xing is disqualified as 'language-less' – it is gibberish rather than language. 'Language-less' is a term used in Blommaert et al. (2005a: 210) to describe a Bulgarian immigrant woman who is labelled as 'speaking no language' by local mainly Dutch-speaking people. Here the gibberish noise made by Jun is a similar observation. The analysis between lines 18 and 24 should take into consideration my use of 'us' in line 17 and my 'laughing voice' in line 23, and be cautious that these may signal proving and encouraging attitudes from me on Jun's comments towards Xing. However, throughout the transcript, we can still see how Xing's language is evaluated and disqualified, and how she is grouped into a community of 'non-Beijing speakers', through the identity discourses articulated by her local counterpart on the metapragmatic level – the second level of the general framework. One may wonder how Xing and Jun can still get along with each other and 'had a lot of interaction in-and-out-of class' when Jun is rather discriminating. It is worth mentioning here that Jun also sings praises of Xing every now and then about her being an easy-going person, being helpful to others, and being clever in such subjects as math and drawing. Throughout the semester, I observed many occasions of Jun and Xing being good friends.

Local teacher's metapragmatic discourses and migrant identity construction

Having examined how a local pupil perceives the language and identity of his migrant classmate, let us look at a teacher's evaluations on her migrant pupil's linguistic forms and identity, which have an impact on the performance appraisals of this pupil. Teachers are the powerful party in teacher–pupil relations, whose appraisals of the pupils' performance are often crucial for pupils' academic careers as well as their future development. The following extracts are taken from a feedback interview with Miss Zhang, a Chinese language (*yuwen*) teacher of grade 1 (aged

Scale 2: Metapragmatic Discourses 81

7–8) and a native of Beijing, on a questionnaire about her students' language use and academic performance distributed to her and her colleagues by me at the beginning of the fieldwork. In the feedback interview, she is invited to elaborate the comments she makes and to give examples where necessary.

Example 4.4: 'They think they are Beijing people'

Interview with Miss Zhang in the staff office on 21 June 2007. Hong is a pupil of Miss Zhang.

JD: Oh so Hong is a migrant child; but once I chatted with her and she said she was local, so I had the idea that she is a local...

Miss Zhang: They, well, they, they have all grown up in Beijing, they think they are Beijing people, but actually they are not. They are grade 1 and have no idea who they are; they think they live in Beijing and so they are Beijing people but they are not.

(Fieldwork recording, 2007-06-21-V044)

I go through the questionnaire with Miss Zhang and am surprised that she marked Hong as a migrant child. A few days prior to the interview Hong and I have a talk in which she says that she is a local child and she even goes to a local kindergarten[4] before attending this school. I have no doubt about what she tells me as she speaks with a Beijing accent to my ear. But here her self-ascribed local identity is denied and she is ascribed a 'migrant identity' although she grows up in Beijing and acquires a local accent. In line 3 Miss Zhang emphasises on 'they', in the same way that Jun does in Example 4.3, and extends her comment to the migrant population as a homogeneous community. Being a local person and a teacher, Miss Zhang is in the position to judge Hong's identity and to decide that she is not a local although she herself thought she was. The evaluation of Miss Zhang (MZ) on Hong's language and performance is given below.

1 JD: ... then does she have an accent?
  MZ: She doesn't distinguish '*n*' and '*l*'. People from Sichuan all speak like this. {another teacher interrupted and told a story about her experiences in Sichuan}
5 JD: {pointing to the questionnaire} Well, here, 'her accent has a big impact on her performance', did you mean the '*n*' and '*l*' distinction?

	MZ:	Yes. Her *Pinyin*, you see, tasks such as 'read *Pinyin* and write down words',
10	JD:	she has never done well.
	MZ:	= in Chinese lessons ...
	JD:	= She has difficulties in *Pinyin*.
	MZ:	But her overall remarks are average {pointing to the questionnaire item where Miss Zhang selected the middle one out of a five-
15		point Likert scale} ...
	JD:	Yes average.
	MZ:	So you meant her overall performance?
	JD:	Because pronunciation is only one aspect that influences her study; but things such as her intelligence, her cognitive ability, are quite good which make up for it.
	MZ:	Otherwise she could do better (in the evaluation) ... Exactly.

(Fieldwork recording, 2007-06-21-V045)

Analysis and interpretation

Having noted Miss Zhang's comments on Hong's identity, I interviewed her about Hong's language. Miss Zhang mentioned that a linguistic characteristic of Hong is the lack of distinction between dental nasal [n] and dental lateral [l]. It is uncertain to me whether it is an influence of accent or a result of unclear pronunciation[5] that is particularly common among children of this age. Miss Zhang perceives Sichuan dialect speakers as a uniform community characterised by this linguistic feature 'People from Sichuan all speak like this' in lines 2 and 3. Later I ask Miss Zhang whether there are regional differences in the linguistic features among the migrant pupils in her class and she responds that she does not think there are salient differences – 'I didn't notice much difference' (Fieldwork recording, 2007-06-21-V045). Why does Miss Zhang on the one hand comment that all Sichuan native speakers share the feature of undistinguishing [n] and [l], but on the other, notices little differences among the regional varieties?

This is not difficult to understand if we look at it from a language ideology point of view: The information she gives reflects the language ideology that self-evidently marks Putonghua as the correct language. The feature of not distinguishing between [n] and [l] is an 'incorrect' feature, measured against Putonghua in the educational arena, and dialects that have this feature are therefore 'incorrect' speech varieties. Given the specific position of Beijing Mandarin – being the original form of Putonghua – the Putonghua spoken by Beijing people is often believed to be standard, accent-less and uncontaminated, whereas the Putonghua of someone like Hong is accented, and to be corrected (but both Beijing Mandarin and Putonghua are of course accents, and indeed very remarkable accents). The distinction is drawn between Putonghua and dialects, and the overwhelming linguistic differences among dialects become invisible (or 'erasure' in Irvine & Gal's (2000: 38) term – dominant ideologies making some features of reality invisible). In our case of Miss Zhang's evaluation, the languages of migrants are considered as homogeneous, and its variation is disregarded and ignored.

One small feature of language has become emblematic of individual and group identities, and the migrant identity, ascribed to Hong, has amplified the linguistic feature – it might have gone unnoticed if this particular phonetic mix happened in the speech of a Beijing child. But here Hong is labelled as a migrant child and thus 'her accent has a big impact on her performance' in line 5. She marks it '4' on the five-point Likert scale. Her interview elaboration on the questionnaire choice, however, shows that the negative impact is perhaps very limited. She mentions that tasks such as 'read *Pinyin* and write down words' are negatively influenced by Hong's accent (lines 7 and 8). Figure 4.1 is an example of such tasks.

The first line in bold is the instruction of the task: 'read *Pinyin* and write down words'; *Pinyin* is given above every square-shaped blank, and corresponding characters are supposed to be filled in the squares. Unable to distinguish [n] and [l] may be a 'problem' in Hong's Chinese, but not in her other subjects nor her intellectual capacities; it is limited to the use of *Pinyin*, and does not affect other aspects of her Chinese such as grammar. Even in the use of *Pinyin*, the damage of the absence of [n]/[l] distinction is actually limited, because one Chinese character rarely stands on its own; a word in Chinese often consists of two or more characters. If a pupil

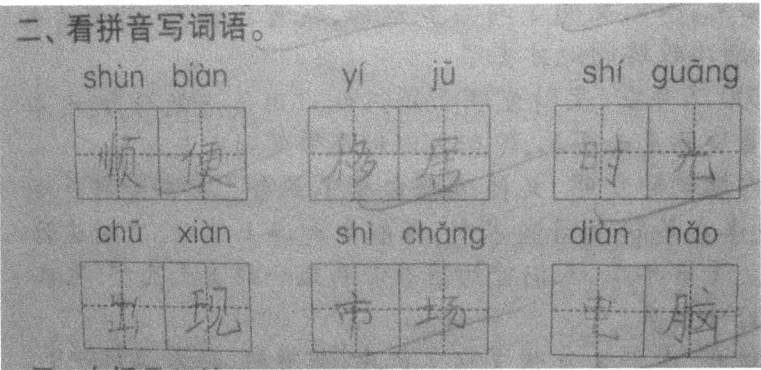

Figure 4.1 An example of 'reading *Pinyin* and write down words' task

is uncertain about the consonant of one character, he or she still has a chance to get the word right because of the cue from the other character in the word. Nevertheless, migrant pupils can have lower than average performance in this kind of task that specifically tests their mastery of the 'standard' *pronunciation*; however, this should not have a 'big impact' on a pupil's performance, as Miss Zhang indicates in the questionnaire.

From lines 11 to 15 Miss Zhang comments on Hong's general performance and points out that Hong is intelligent and cognitively able to achieve good learning results. If she spoke 'better language' she could have received a better general appraisal from the school. It is safe to say from the interview that the linguistic features of the migrant child influence the appraisal she receives. The migrant child is different, as she speaks differently; the differences index identities of being rural, lower working class and migrant. Within the monoglot language ideology, all these indexicalities are not made explicit; it simply takes the form of being 'incorrect'. Her language is 'incorrect' – not distinguishing [n] and [l] results in her failing of *pinyin* tasks. She should replace her 'mistakes' with the 'correct' language, otherwise her performance would be negatively influenced by the 'incorrect' language.

The evaluation of Hong's performance is done in a seemingly neutral way, with recognition of her cognitive ability, and indeed in many occasions I observe support and encouragements from both local teachers and pupils towards migrant children in the school. This interview, however, demonstrates that Hong's language plays a role in the appraisal and as her teacher points out, she could be a 'better' student if she spoke the 'correct' language. Why does the interview result not fit into the general observation? This may be answered by applying the notion of scaling in our explanation. When the teacher recognises Hong's intellectual capacity, expresses support and encouragement to the migrant pupil, she functions from an interpersonal scale of teacher–pupil interactions. In contrast, she talks from an institutional scale on student performance appraisals when articulating the 'problems' of migrant pupils' linguistic features, their identities and their academic performances. The practices of the teacher at these two scales are not contradictory or exclusive to each other. Chapter 5 will take this issue further.

Summary

This chapter has shown the construction of migrant identities on the scale of metapragmatic linguistic practice through four examples of identity making discourse by migrant pupils, their local Beijing counterparts and their teachers. The central concepts deployed for this chapter are ethnolinguistic identity and speech community. It also draws on the concepts addressed in the previous chapters, such as indexicality, scale, space and monoglot ideology. The monoglot language ideology in China often revolves around Putonghua, an association that feeds into the 'one language-one culture' assumption and results in an imagined singular, clear and stable ethnolinguistic identity. In the actual linguistic exchanges, however, the one-to-one relationship is blurred when we observe that multiple 'languages', 'dialects' or 'accents' are organised as a linguistic repertoire of migrants, that various speech communities share one 'language', and such communities are defined in relation to the sharedness of indexical values.

The application of these concepts in the analyses of the four examples has shed light on the metapragmatic processes of migrant identity construction. In the first example, I observe a drawing class at a Beijing primary school during which a migrant pupil articulates a metapragmatic discourse on her own and her fellow-pupil's identities, and overlays their migrant identities with a national identity through a scale-jumping move. This self-claimed ethnolinguistic identity in the first example is questioned in the second example that documents a group discussion on home languages and dialects among migrant pupils. The migrant children's metapragmatic comments disqualifies their linguistic repertoires and naturalises Putonghua as the language for the social space. A Beijing pupil, in contrast, is named to be an exemplary dialect speaker precisely because she escapes the identities of being a native dialect speaker and migrant child.

The 'taken-for-granted' disposition takes the shape of an orientation towards Putonghua in the first and second examples, and this is echoed in the third and the fourth examples, both of which are metapragmatic discourses on migrant pupils' languages and identities. Meanwhile, the blurring of migrant and local identities in the first example is challenged in the second example and denied in the third and the fourth examples. The third example shows the comments of a local Beijing pupil on his migrant fellow-pupil's accent: The accent indexed her identities of being of rural origin and a migrant to the city. The fourth example examines a teacher's comments on her pupil's identity, language and performance.

Metapragmatic discourses, the second level of the general theoretical framework of this study, make identity construction explicit. People articulate identity evaluations and classify themselves as well as others into discursively constructed social categories. Identities claimed by oneself at the first level of the general framework – the linguistic exchange level – are ratified, negotiated or challenged by others at the scale of metapragmatic discourse. At this scale, we also observe that the identity of being a 'migrant' is often ascribed and imposed by others; the third and fourth examples instantiate this observation. In short, the identities constructed at the metapragmatic discourse scale are less fluid compared to the linguistic communicative scale analysed in Chapter 3. Although the data are collected from very different social settings (the examples in Chapter 3 are mainly from migrant neighbourhoods, whereas the examples of this chapter are all from a school, a scale-defining institution itself), we can still see that the identity construction of this high-scale evaluation – the metapragmatic discourse scale – involves the ascription and categorisation of others. In the following chapter, we shall see that identities become more rigid and categorical when our attention moves further up to the public and institutional scale, and discourses produced on this scale often invoke general social norms and administrative realities.

Notes

1. An earlier version of this chapter, titled 'Isn't It Enough to be a Chinese Speaker': Language Ideology and Migrant Identity Construction in a Public Primary School in Beijing', is published in *Language & Communication* 29(2): 115–126.
2. There are eight administrative districts in central Beijing and 10 on the outskirts of the city.
3. *wai di ren*, literally 'other place people', refers to anyone who comes from places other than a speaker's locality within the country.
4. Urban kindergartens are often unaffordable to many migrant families because pre-school care is not part of compulsory education and does not receive government subsidy in the way that primary schools do. Kindergartens are mostly operated for profit in Beijing.
5. What we call *da she tou*, in Chinese, literally 'big tongue'; I have come across quite a number of Beijing children who were called *da she tou* because they do not distinguish between *n* and *l* at this age (around seven and eight years old) and later adjusted themselves.

Chapter 5
Scale 3: Institutions

Introduction

This chapter extends the argument developed in the previous chapters in exploring the discursive processes of migrant identity construction on the third scale – the public and institutional discourse scale. This scale deals with discourses produced and circulated in the public and institutional spheres, such as media reports, online debates, government policies, institutional regulations and so forth. Such discourses, although being diversified in both form and content, share a common feature: they lead us into a space in which people invoke administrative notions of identity categorisation and general rules of social conduct. In this space identity categories are rigid, static, stereotypical and general.

We are thus facing forms of identity that are different in type from the ones we highlighted in Chapters 3 and 4. Identities in this chapter appear solid, uncompromising, not negotiable and categorical. What we observe in identity discourses on this scale is not always a matter of choice or a creative deployment of linguistic resources; rather, both discourse choices and identity negotiations are constrained by normativities, that is, the general patterns in the dimension of social organisations. People do make a choice of linguistic resources creatively, as shown in the street vendor case (Example 3.3), but there is always a limit to choice (Blommaert, 2005a). On the third scale of the general framework, we encounter very clearly defined and strictly categorised identifications such as 'asylum seekers', 'economic immigrants', 'EU-passport holders' and so forth in the Western European contexts (Extra *et al.*, 2009). In our case of Chinese internal migrants, the decisive line is drawn between rural and urban residents, and although such a distinction is in many ways diminishing and in many circumstances invisible, it is indisputably printed in one's *hukou* (see section 'Identity and Identity Studies'). One is either a rural *hukou*-holder or an urban *hukou*-holder, and to a large extent, this distinction conditions what one can get in one's daily life. Such administrative categorisations can, of course, enter interactional events. They can be the outcome of, for instance, service encounters or encounters with the authorities, or they can be the input of such interactions (Briggs, 1997; Maryns, 2006). They are not entirely separated from the interactional dynamics discussed in the previous chapters. Yet, it is important to underline the specificity of the kind of identities we discuss here: they are not individual but categorical, and held to be dominant (i.e. of a general validity that overrides the particularities of individual cases), and rooted in the big structure of society. They consequently also operate through different kinds of discourses: discourses in the public sphere, institutional discourses and administrative discourses.

In what follows, I first introduce the central notions of this chapter, that is, 'abnormality', 'stigma' and 'modernity'. I review the theorisation and application of these notions in Western European and Northern American contexts, and discuss the possibility of their usage in the present research. My focus then moves on to the analysis and interpretation of three examples illustrating the identity construction on the third scale. At the end of the chapter, I offer a summary and return to the three-scale general framework.

Central Concepts: Abnormality, Stigma and Modernity

The central concepts for this chapter reflect their object. We are addressing general patterns of identity attribution, and in contrast to the more immediately operational concepts in the previous chapters, the concepts we use here are more general, and aimed at providing a perspective rather then an analytical technique. The term 'abnormality' has appeared a couple of times in this book: in Chapter 3, the Sichuan pupil's accent was 'an "abnormal" accent, bespeaking an "abnormal" identity' (Example 3.1), and in Chapter 4 the home dialects of migrant pupils were abnormalised through such descriptions as 'funny', 'terrible', 'foreign' (Example 4.2). The notion of 'abnormal' is borrowed from Foucault's *Abnormal* (2003), an edition of his lectures at the Collège de France between 1974 and 1975. Foucault's work *Abnormal* as well as his other studies on power, knowledge and the historical formation of modern institutions, provide rich theoretical references for conceptualising and analysing discourse and power in society. The relevance of *Abnormal* for my research on language and migrant identity needs to be seen in the light that Foucault's work is a 'diagnostic' analysis of contemporary French society coupled with an understanding of how it came into being (Blommaert, 2005a). In the current study, the 'abnormal individual' is understood as 'the individual who cannot be integrated within the normative system of education' (Foucault, 2003: 291). The peculiarity of abnormality lies in its introduction of disorder to and its disruption of the normative system. The norm is the rule of conduct, the tacit law, the principle of order and conformity, against which irregularity, disorder, disorganisation, dysfunction, deviation are measured and disqualified (Foucault, 2003: 162). Essential to my research, 'abnormality' is 'ab-normality', something that deviates from 'normal', producing someone who is to be corrected.

Foucault's 'abnormal individual' is a historical figure formed in correlation with and so generated by the institutional control and surveillance of modernity. In face-to-face interactions, a useful notion germane to 'abnormality' can be found in Goffman's *Stigma* (1974b), in which the stigmatised individual is defined as the one who falls short of our 'normative expectations', and a stigma is an 'undesired differentness' as opposed to the *'normal'* (Goffman, 1974b: 2–5, italics in original). The notion of stigma has been used in various places of the present study, such as in the Sichuan child case and in the drawing class case (Example 4.1). In Goffman's elaboration of this notion, stigma can be a physical deformity, a mental blemish such as imprisonment, alcoholism, the asocial and unemployment, and a 'tribal' stigma of race, nation, religion, social class. Moreover, the adolescent, the light-skinned black people, the second-generation immigrant are stigmatised in the sense that one is uncertain of how 'we normals will identify him and receive him' (Goffman, 1974b: 13). What is particularly relevant to my study is that the rural–urban migrant worker bears the physical stigma of speaking and behaving differently from the local, the mental stigma of having an undesired identity and the 'tribal' stigma (in Goffman's term) of being of a lower social class. The three forms of stigma combine in a general image of the migrant as 'abnormal'.

Furthermore, the stigmatised individual is expected to take the stance of the normal and to normalise himself by seeing himself as 'essentially' normal and 'as a fully human being like anyone else' (Goffman, 1974b: 115). He who is able to do so is considered to have achieved a good personal adjustment, but he who is unable to do so is associated with such features as being self-isolated, suspicious, depressed, bewildered, hostile, in short, as being an impaired person with inadequate inner resources. This can be instantiated by a fieldwork recording of a migrant teacher's comments on her migrant pupils:

> They (the migrant pupils) are too sensitive of what Beijing people say and do, it might be okay if we who were also migrants said the same

thing, but it would be a problem (if that was said by a local people). They are over sensitive. (Fieldwork recording, 2007-06-11-V026)

According to the teacher's comments, the migrant pupils were qualified as 'over sensitive', a characteristic ranked among 'being self-isolated', 'depressed', 'bewildered' and so on, which was resulted from their incapacity of seeing themselves as 'essentially normal' as the local. Along this line of arguments, the 'problem' between the local and the migrant was not generated by the attitudes of the local towards the migrant, but by migrant workers' inability of achieving adequate personal adjustment, and by their 'inadequate inner resources'. Similar to what Goffman says, '[n]ormals really mean no harm; when they do, it is because they don't know better. They should therefore be tactfully helped to act nicely' (Goffman, 1974b: 116). The teacher's comments seem to suggest that the migrant pupils should 'help' the normal – the local people – by being 'less sensitive' and by achieving a 'good personal adjustment'.

The notion of abnormality and that of stigma have been theorised in different social contexts (Western Europe and North America), in relation to different disciplines (psychiatry and sociology), and on different levels of investigation (historical and interactional). The significance of both notions for my study, however, lies in the social construction of the normal as opposed to the abnormal and the stigmatised. Both notions conceptualise deviation from normality, and both describe the 'disorderly' individual who does not fit into the order, who displays features of 'not orderly', who needs to be mainstreamed.

'Order' is the defining social product of modernity, and to maintain an orderly world is the eternal task of modernity (Bauman, 1991). An orderly world is a world in which we know how to go on, where to find out, what we can foresee of the future based on our knowledge and experience of the past. Modernity (not to be confused with 'modernism', cf. Bauman, 1991: 4) is a historical period in Western Europe and later North America. It is marked by a series of intellectual and social transformations starting in the 17th century – intellectually, the Enlightenment, and socially, the rise of industrial society and industrial capitalism. Some theorists argue that the modern era has ended and we are now in an era of postmodernity; others believe that we are in late-modernity, 'liquid' modernity or still in 'high' modernity (see Anderson, 1998; Bauman, 1991; Giddens, 1990, 1991; Harvey, 1990). A comprehensive review of these debates is beyond the scope of my study. Instead, I would suggest that the major instruments of modernity are still in place: first, the basis of modernity – clear administratively and bureaucratically structured modern nation-states; second, the power of modern system – the institutional control and surveillance on individual rights and duties; and third, the pursuit of order – that is, to classify, to define, and to structure the world according to clear and generally valid categories (see for example Blommaert, 2009c). At the centre of modernity, argues Foucault, is the distinction between 'abnormality' and 'normality'. The abnormal individual brings disorder into the orderly world, the order is broken by his presence, and he is to be normalised so as to fit the order.

This chapter studies the identity making on the public and institutional scale. Discourses produced on this scale often invoke rigid general social norms and administrative categorisations. On this scale we encounter talk from the 'top', talks that are not restricted to a single case, but is seen to have general validity, and is believed to be applicable to every member of the social category. A phenomenon often observed on this scale is that migrant identity is presented as an aberrant identity, an individual that brings disorder to the urban social norms, through such discourses as 'we have too many immigrants', and 'it is dangerous to enter that immigrant area'. The category of 'migrant' at this scale is inflated and covers features of social class, regional background, ethnicity, language and (as we shall see) everyday aspects of behaviour such as dress. The essential connections between the central concepts and the public and institutional scale lie in the distinction between normality and abnormality or stigma rigidly defined in the public and institutional sphere discourses that are grounded in the administratively orderly modern world. Different from the central notions introduced in the previous chapters, the notions of this chapter are not as operational in data analysis and interpretation, but provide us with a perspective in understanding the identity making dynamics on the public and institutional scale.

The central notions of this chapter are theorised in dramatically different social contexts from that of China, and are used primarily in disciplines other than discourse analysis and sociolinguistics. Therefore this chapter is certainly exploratory in the sense that it attempts to apply these notions in the discursive process of identity construction in the Chinese context. In this attempt, the notion of 'abnormal' has definitely moved away from Foucault's penal psychiatry analysis, but emphasised its fundamental meaning of 'ab-normal', something that does not fit into the normative system.

Abnormal Identities

The data I discuss come from different sources and are themselves of very different natures – some of them came from my fieldwork sites (the schools), others from newspapers, periodicals, the internet, policy papers and so on. Some of the data are interviews on school regulations, and others are documentation. The common themes that synthesise the data of this chapter, however, are the scale on which they are produced and circulated – the public and institutional discourse – and the particularity of identities they construct – rigid, inflexible, stereotypical and abstract – in relation to the discourses on the communicative and the metapragmatic scales. We now enter a world of public discourses in which general social norms and administrative realities are being invoked, and we shall see that this space has rules of its own.

'Learn Putonghua before migration'

The first example (Example 5.1) we consider is an extract of a small article accompanied by a cartoon (see Appendix 2 for the original text in Chinese). The article appeared in a monthly periodical called *Nongmin Keji Peixun* (*Science and Technology Training for Farmers*, 2005), published by a training centre of the Ministry of Agriculture.[1] This periodical has a readership of rural residents and people who work in agriculture-related sectors. The title of this article is *Jincheng wugong qian lianhao Putonghua* (*Practising Putonghua well before entering the city and searching for jobs*, Fig. 5.1), published in the section *Nomgmingong Zhi Jia* (*A Home for Migrant Workers*). The author of this article is anonymous.

Example 5.1: 'Learning Putonghua before entering the city'

Figure 5.1 The cartoon for the article *Practising Putonghua well before entering the city and searching for jobs*

1 ... it is extremely urgent (for migrant workers) to practice and to
achieve a good level of Putonghua proficiency before entering
cities and searching for jobs; otherwise it would be very difficult
for you even to move around in the urban areas. It is evident that
5 Putonghua is a barrier for rural redundant labourers to find jobs
in cities. If (one) speaks good Putonghua, one will not only give
a good impression (to others) in job interviews and thus increase
one's employability; one can communicate with people
effectively, express oneself clearly ... so that one can find a good
10 job and settle in the city. If what one said could not be
understood by others, even if he might be excellent in his job, he
could not communicate with those around him, others might feel
that he was not trustworthy, and this would therefore diminish
his competitiveness. Meanwhile, the language barrier prevents
15 one from communicating with others, and hence makes him
isolated, and his emotional needs would be hardly satisfied ...

Analysis and interpretation

This article is written for general use by the public. It is a multimodal document combining both visual and textual signs (Kress & van Leeuwen, 1996). It targets rural residents who have not yet migrated but intend to leave their farming land for urban employment, and it stresses the importance of Putonghua in job hunting, in raising their chance of eventual settlement in cities and in enhancing their quality of life. The most striking feature of the discourse is the visual cartoon illustration that immediately grasps the reader's attention. The cartoon depicts a social encounter of a couple and a young man. The couple, on the left-hand side, is in old-fashioned tops with traditional Chinese style collar and rag shoes; they have their sleeves and trousers folded as if they are ready to work; they carry much luggage; they have an innocent smile and an optimistic look on their faces – all these visual cues imply that they are on the move from their country-side home with a hope of a better life in the city. The rural couple is on the boundary of a city – they are standing against a flat landscape of plants, whereas the background on the side of the young man is filled with high-rise buildings, factories and skyscrapers. The young man, clearly an urban character, shod in leather and dressed in a lapel jacket, is talking to the couple while pointing towards the city. Note the different facial expression he has as opposed to that of the migrant couple – this is a confident look, related to a voice of authority which can tell the country couple what they should do and where they can go, if they do not speak good Putonghua, in the city. The reader could hence imagine that the young man speaks standard Putonghua whereas the migrant couple does not.

This visual representation parallels the text, which reflexively formulates Putonghua as a tool of communication and of successful employment. Putonghua, thus, is a marker of 'normality', and not speaking it is a marker of 'abnormality'. In lines 1–8, it establishes the importance of acquiring Putonghua ('it is extremely urgent', lines 1 and 2), and this claim is reinforced in lines 9 and 10 that migrants cannot move around in cities if they do not speak Putonghua. The urban areas, uniformly defined as opposed to 'the rural areas', are practically guarded by Putonghua, and people who do not speak it are reduced to be dysfunctional or functionless – abnormal – in cities. In terms of employment, the text suggests, Putonghua is self-evidently a 'barrier' (line 11) for migrant workers: people who master this 'tool' well can impress the potential employer in a positive way and increase their employability (lines 12–15), because it enables them to 'communicate with people effectively', and to express themselves clearly. People who do not speak Putonghua well, however, are negatively qualified – stigmatised – in various ways: 'he could not communicate with those around him', he is seen as 'untrustworthy', he is not competitive although he 'might be excellent in his job', and finally, he may feel 'isolated' in cities because he cannot talk with others (lines 16–22). Note the dense clustering of 'abnormal' character features attached to 'poor' Putonghua from lines 16 to 22, in contrast to an image of the ideal urban subject – someone who looks and sounds trustworthy, competitive and confident. As such, a huge number of dialects and vernaculars are collectively abnormalised, and the migrant worker with inadequate Putonghua proficiency becomes an abnormal figure who is 'suspicious' both in individual integrity and in employability.

This article is produced by an unnamed author of an affiliated training centre of China's Ministry of Agriculture. Although the author's voice is not necessarily that of the Ministry, the stance of this article is nevertheless in line with the officially and institutionally endorsed one, that is, stressing the importance of using Putonghua as a common tool of communication and urging those who are not yet proficient in speaking Putonghua to 'improve' and to 'correct' their language for the sake of their own benefit and well-being.[2] The article is circulated in the public domain, and in the meantime it circulates an ideal urban image of being capable, reliable, sociable, smartly dressed, mentally healthy, physically mobile, possessing the 'normal' accent and having an optimistic career outlook – in short, a 'normal' member of the mainstream society. It draws a neat line between this ideal urban individual and the potential migrant worker, the reader of this article. This demarcation is portrayed in the visual sign and is explicitly described in the text. The reader could easily perceive the earnestness of the text in offering practical advice to young farmers who are preparing themselves to take the step of leaving home for cities. Given the enormous sociolinguistic diversity of China, it would be difficult for someone who speaks only his regional vernacular to communicate with others to whom the vernacular is unintelligible; Putonghua is thus elevated to the position of lingua franca in its function of providing a common platform for communication.

Beneath this practical layer of advice-giving, however, we could unearth a deeper level of meaning conveyed by the text: The potential migrant worker speaks an abnormal accent or dialect, which invokes not only rigid administrative notions of 'migrant worker' who risks disrupting the orderly modern world, and who is therefore to be educated and mainstreamed, but also the general social norms of speaking the standard language that defines the normal urban citizen and the urban space. On this scale of public and institutional discourse, the migrant identities become inflexible and stereotypical: The migrant worker dresses like the cartoon couple, moves around with much luggage, speaks a vernacular and is frequently in-and-out of jobs. The identity making discourses on this scale are often impressionist; these discourses are not about a specific case, but refer to migrant workers at a general level, and consequently migrant identities made in such general discourses are static and abstract. I take this point further in the next example.

'Change clothes before getting on the bus'

The public sphere discourses are traditionally found in newspapers, magazines, radio broadcastings and TV programmes, such as the one we have seen in Example 5.1. The invention and popularisation of the internet, a remarkable phenomenon of globalisation, increasingly provide people with an electronically mediated platform of information exchange and communication. In addition, the internet has restructured the public space, notably through new genres such as the web forum, the 'Facebook' phenomenon and the blog. In all these cases private voices become publicly available, and we get new genres of public information exchange that defy traditional definitions of 'mass media'. The discussion of identity construction on the third scale draws rich data from this relatively recent yet widely spread form of public discourse. Let us look at some of these data.

The following example is an online news report about an incident between eight migrant construction workers and a bus driver plus several passengers that happened on 11 January 2009 in a city of the Pearl Delta Region. The news report attracts much public attention and is soon cited by various websites, mainly internet forums and personal web-blogs for discussions and debates. I first present the translation of the news story, and second, present the development of the web forum debates by listing thirteen entries. I focus on Response (50) in the analysis and interpretation.

Example 5.2: '... but after all it was your fault ...'

1   On 11 January 2009, in a city of the Pearl Delta Region, migrant
    construction worker Mr Cai and seven of his co-workers took a
    bus. The bus driver and some passengers required Mr Cai and
    his colleagues to change clothes, because their clothes – the
5   overalls for construction work – were covered with wet paint
    and dust. The two sides had an argument, and Mr Cai rang the
    bus operation company to complain. He was informed via phone
    about the bus company regulation that people who wore
    besmearing clothes (clothes that potentially besmear others'
10 clothes or the public environment of a bus) should not get on a
    bus. Mr Cai indicated that he and his co-workers initially felt
    sorry that they had to wore stained overalls on the bus; but they
    felt that the way the bus driver and the passengers spoke was
    discriminating and insulting, which led to an argument. The bus
15 driver said that he did not discriminate against Mr Cai and his
    co-workers; the bus was very crowded and he had to act for the
    sake of other passengers. He believed that the construction
    workers misunderstood him and that this had led to the row

People responded with divergent comments. In the following list of debate entries, the most frequently voiced opinions were to stress the equality between migrant workers and urban citizens, the right of migrant workers to use the public transport system and their freedom to choose what to wear:[3]

Response (4):   I think everyone is equal.
Response (5):   A bus is a public transport tool, every citizen has the right to use it.
                Every citizen has the freedom to wear (what he wants to) ...
Response (7):   It wouldn't be a problem if (the bus driver) spoke in a nice way.

Scale 3: Institutions

Response (8):   Everyone should be treated equally.
Response (9):   Agree.

Many responses show sympathy towards migrant workers and indicate that the bus driver's way of treating the migrant workers is discriminating:

Response (26):   Serious discrimination, outrageous.
Response (60):   They (migrant workers) do the most unwanted jobs and live on the lowest wages, they have no social welfare and security (in the city), they are far away from their homes and families, they are the socially disadvantaged, you may not be sympathetic to them, but at least don't discriminate against them, try not to insult others.

Some responses, however, blame both parties for the incident, for example:

Response (67):   Can't (the bus driver and the passengers) speak in a friendly way? Attitude!! And it would be nothing if the migrant workers were more conscious (about how to behave).
Response (147):   Although (people) have the right to use the public transport, (they) also have the obligation to respect the public order, and the public hygiene standard. People who do not fulfil their obligation can not realise their right.

People who are on the side of the bus driver and the urban passengers argue:

Response (149):   I don't think it is discrimination, when it rains, we should take off wet raincoats and fold umbrellas whiling taking a bus, it is the same (that people should take off their dirty work wears in bus).
Response (20):   In public areas, (people) should be considerate to others ... it is the same in nature with the no-smoking rule in public space, if you want a smoke, (you) have to go outside and smoke, is this a discrimination?! ...

The following response is also on the side of the bus driver. I give it additional attention and list it separately because of its interesting visual and textual combination. This response (Response 50) argues against Response (5) (Fig. 5.2):

(The sentence in smaller font on top of Response (50) is its citation of Response (5))

1   **Response (50):** you have the right to wear (any) kind of clothes and to take a bus, but you don't have the right to make others'

clothes dirty, if you do, others have the right to require you to clean (their clothes), in other countries they would send you their
5   dry cleaning bills, don't challenge the rights of the public with your own so called right, whenever it is, the ultimate aim of the law is to protect the rights of the public, you may feel unfairly treated, but after all it was your own fault, you knew that you had to take a bus, and you knew that your clothes were dirty,
10 why didn't you try to clean them, or to bring other clothes with you for change, you knew clearly that you would make others' clothes dirty (in such a crowded bus), you still asserted that you were discriminated, what your moral standard was, you didn't respect others in the first place, and therefore others didn't have
15 the obligation to respect you ... there is nothing you deserve, win respect with your own effort!

In the prefinal line there is an inverted smiley with signs of contempt. The sentence with a bigger font in the white space says, 'I don't agree with you!!'

The migrant workers are sometimes blamed:

Response (21): ... some people consider themselves to be the disadvantaged, to be the target of discrimination, although people raise reasonable requirements to them, these people would claim that they are discriminated – this is no good, first, these people should not look down upon themselves, they should adjust their own attitudes (they should believe that) people respect each other, everyone should observe social moral value and social order.

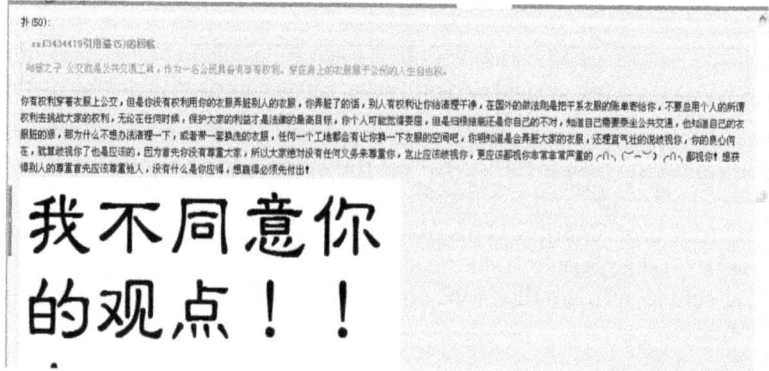

Figure 5.2 Response 50

Scale 3: Institutions

Analysis and interpretation

Let us take a close look at the news story and the responses. The news story describes an interaction between eight migrant workers and a bus driver. The migrant construction workers wore dirty overalls in a crowded bus. The bus drivers and some passengers required the migrant workers to change clothes; the migrant workers, who worked with paint, cement and other building materials in a construction site, felt that they were discriminated against and complained to the bus company. The company regulation, however, stated that passengers should not wear smearing clothes in the bus. It is unclear as to what was said and how the bus driver and the passengers talked to Mr Cai and his colleagues, but according to the news report, the incident was a 'row', or translated more literally, a 'minor conflict'. We could thus imagine that both the form and the content of the interaction were not terribly pleasant. The incident might seem accidental; however, the fact that it attracted much public attention and debates (thanks to the internet which makes private voices public), suggests that it was hardly an isolated accident, but rather an expression of the increasingly tense relationship between urban citizens and migrant workers. Behind this synchronic event, we see the underlying social structure and the gradual but remarkable structural changes, among which the rise of migrant workers as a social stratum, and the abnormalisation and stigmatisation of migrant social identities in the urban space, here, articulated around their physical appearance. They are (low-paid) construction workers, and they look like that.

Did the bus driver and the passengers discriminate against the migrant workers? Was it a moral problem of the migrant workers? Was the bus company regulation discriminating? Many internet forums and blogs post the news story and raise these questions for online debates. It is virtually impossible to include all websites that offer discussions on this incident; the one I choose as the data source, 'mop.com', is one of the most widely used online forums in China. It is also difficult to include all responses; to give a balanced view of – the debates, I organise the opinions into three groups:

- Those on the side of Mr Cai and his colleagues.
- Those blaming both for the incident.
- Those on the side of the bus driver and the passengers.

There are five examples of the responses in support of Mr Cai and his co-workers. The arguments focus on the equality of people, on the migrant workers' right of using the public transport system and on people's fundamental freedom in choosing what they wear. These arguments are often brief, such as one sentence, a few words or just one word, yet they are frequently featured viewpoints, and they usually appear at the beginning of an online debate. Responses (4), (5), (7), (8) and (9) are of this group; in fact, the first 20 responses are dominated by this stance. These features may suggest that this stance is straightforward, an intuitive reaction on hearing about the incident.

Response (26) is an example of explicitly criticising discrimination and expressing anger toward the discriminatory behaviour. As the discussion goes deeper, people start looking at issues behind the incident itself; for example, Response (60) points out that migrant workers are a socially disadvantaged group who have to leave their families behind and come to the city for those jobs that are avoided by urban people; they live just above the urban minimal income line; they cannot afford becoming ill in the city because their social welfare and security is linked to their *hukou* locality, which means that they have to go back to their hometown for medical treatment.[4] This response calls for sympathy towards migrant workers, and similar to Response (26), it criticises the discriminating attitudes towards migrant workers.

Response (67) is an example of the opinion group that blames both sides for the incident. It points out that the attitudes of the bus driver and the passengers might have caused the incident, that it would not have been a problem if they had spoken to the migrant workers in a friendly way. It also blames the migrant workers for not being conscious and mindful of their behaviour in the public space. Response (147) affirms the migrant workers' right in using the public transport system, but it seems to place more emphasis on their 'obligation to respect the public order and the public hygiene'. The term 'public order' is used here to refer to such tacit rules as queuing at the bus stand, standing on the right-hand side while taking a escalator, talking to each other in a low voice inside a museum and so on, and in our case, not wearing stained work overalls in a crowded bus. These are often norms that are tacitly taken for granted in the urban space, and people who fail to obey these norms are linked with such descriptions as 'rude', 'uncivilised' or 'abnormal'. What is not taken into consideration is that people in other spaces, such as the countryside, organise their life around different norms. In the urban space, structured around the urban rules of social conducts, the norms of the migrant workers are effectively misrecognised and erased, and consequently their social conduct is abnormalised against the social order. Response (147) says, '[p]eople who do not fulfil their obligation can not realise their right', that is, people who do not fit the order – dressed in work attire that potentially makes others' clothes dirty inside a crowded bus – should not take the bus. Although taking a relatively neutral stance and blaming both sides, Response (147) seems to be more critical towards the migrant workers than towards the bus driver.

Responses (149) and (20) are on the side of the bus driver and compare this incident with two other situations: wearing wet raincoats in the bus and smoking in public places. The no-smoking policy is a widely accepted norm, and although putting away wet rain gear in the bus is not as widely practiced, urban people nevertheless behave in accordance with this unspoken rule. Relating to the two hypothesised situations leads to two points of argument. First, the two situations and the stained work attire case are all about the norms that sustain modern society, and if it is not discriminating to ban smoking and to put away wet rain gear on the bus, it is also not discriminating to demand that stained work clothes should be taken off. Second, these rules are applicable to urban people as well as to rural people, which implies that urban and rural people are treated on an equal basis. These arguments, using the technique of analogy, place emphasis on the 'normal' way of behaviour in the urban public space – it is just normal to refrain from smoking in public places, normal to put away wet umbrellas and normal to take off stained work wear upon going on a bus; those who do not fit this order, whose behaviour deviates from the 'normal', are to be corrected.

Response (50) shows strong emotion by using a remarkably bigger font size and a different font type for the sentence in the white space. It argues against the opinion of Response (5) quoted in grey colour on top of this message, which says 'A bus is a public transport tool, every citizen has the right to use it. Every citizen has the freedom to wear (what he wants to)'. The sentence in the white space reads 'I don't agree with you!!' Being put in a much bigger size and a different font, and located in a white space in contrast to the shallow grey background of the rest, it is an image as well as a text. The text consumer has to combine visual and textual techniques in decoding this image. This multimodal sign implies a strong feeling of the text author against the opinion of Response (5). The use of a double exclamation mark confirms this interpretation. This visual part of Response (50) can be seen as the declaration that attracts the reader's attention to its textual part.

The textual part of Response (50), translated from lines 1 through 15, is in the same size and font as that of other messages. It uses the second person pronoun 'you' throughout the text referring to the migrant workers Mr Cai and his colleagues. The use of the second person pronoun, instead of the commonly used third person pronoun, makes the statement a direct address to the migrant workers and adds to the message a flavour of reproach. Refuting Response (5), this argument is also based on the relationships between rights and obligations ('you have the right to wear (any) clothes and to take a bus'), and between individual rights and collective rights ('you don't have the right to make others' clothes dirty, if you do, others have the right to require you to clean (their clothes)'). It is striking in Response (50) that 'you' – the migrant workers – and 'others' – people in the urban space – are formulated as two distinctive and contrasting groups: 'your' right of taking a bus, 'your' duty of not making 'others' clothes dirty, and 'others' rights of requiring 'you' to clean their clothes. In this specific case, the 'you' and 'others' distinction is a distinction between the migrant workers on the one hand and the bus driver with his passengers on the other, although one can argue that it is not a distinction between the migrant and the local, or between the rural and the urban, but a distinction between the individual and society, individual rights and collective rights, and these rules are equally applicable to urban citizens. In short, individual (transgressive) behaviour is countered with generic normative statements. As we examine this specific case carefully, we cannot eliminate the very visible factor that the people being reproached are migrant workers. In this discourse of the public scale, the migrant identity is rigidly defined against the also rigidly defined local urban identity, and the fluidity of identity construction on the lower linguistic exchange scale is replaced by abstract and general identity categorisation.

In lines 5 and 6, an imperative or prohibitive expression 'don't challenge the rights of the public with your own so called right' is used to signal a command or a prohibition. When interfering with the 'public right', the migrant workers' right to use public transport is qualified and reduced to the 'so called' right, not a 'real' right. The 'public right', the right of the passengers not to have their clothes stained in an orderly modern world, is not an issue in question. It is guarded by the law (lines 6 and 7), regulations, norms, and other tools of institutional control and surveillance, such as the bus operation company's regulation. It is the migrant workers' fault (line 8) that they are being told off, argues Response (50), for their behaviour is a deviation from the normal patterns of conduct. Consequently, the migrant identity is abnormalised. The abnormality lies not in the 'strangeness' or the 'unusualness' of migrant workers present in cities; they are many in number and they enter into daily encounters with urban citizens. Rather, the abnormality lies in their transgression of the social norms, or, in more general terms, their disorderly conduct in an urban context in which (modern) order is the norm. On the public and institutional scale of which this discourse is circulated, general rules of social conduct are constantly invoked, and the administrative notions of local vs. migrant are rigidly defined identity categorisations.

Sharing the stance of Response (50), Response (21) argues from a different perspective. It states that 'some people' – presumably the migrant workers – believe themselves to be socially disadvantaged, and tend to interpret the reactions they encounter as discriminatory experiences. According to Response (21), even though the requirements of others are 'reasonable', such as changing dirty overalls in order to take a bus, the migrant workers still believe it is a form of discrimination because of (as Response (21) implies) their sense of inferiority. The essential cause of this incident seems to be the attitudes of the migrant workers '... this is no good, first, these people should not look down upon themselves, they should adjust their own attitudes ...'. This argument places the blame on the migrant workers – they have, in the first place, the wrong attitudes towards themselves and towards others, which colour their understanding of the reactions of the bus driver and the passengers. Their misunderstanding, implies Response (21), generates the conflict.

This argument echoes Goffman's (1974b) notion of 'stigmatised identity' – the stigmatised individual is the one who falls short of our normative expectations, who possesses an undesired differentness, such as a physical deformity, an unusual mental state, a racial feature or a trait that turns people whom he meets away from him (Goffman, 1974b: 5). In our case, Mr Cai and his co-workers' behaviour, wearing stained overalls in a crowded bus, is undesirably different from the normal way of urban people's behaviour, which betrays their migrant identity – a *stigmatised* identity. The stigma is not only a stigma about being 'migrants', but also about being 'lower social class': low-paid workers who dress as low-paid workers. The stigmatised individuals, the migrant workers, make their social encounter with the normals – the urban people – difficult because of their lack of 'self-adjustment', according to Response (21). By the same token, what the migrant workers should have done is what Goffman (1974b: 31) calls 'normification' – the effort from the stigmatised individual to 'present himself as an ordinary person', to adjust himself to the way of the normal, and to take the stance of the normal. The migrant workers in this incident, however, do not 'normify' themselves by behaving like the urban, and by observing the social order of the urban space. In short, Response (21) argues that the incident is a result of the migrant workers' stigmatised identity.

My analysis of the internet forum discourses in this example is not about who is right and who is wrong; it is not relevant to decide whether the bus driver should have used a more friendly tone or the migrant workers should have changed their stained work attire while taking a crowded bus; it is not even relevant to make a judgement on whether the bus driver is discriminating or the migrant workers are over-reacting. What I want to show is the abnormalisation and the stigmatisation of the migrant identity in the social encounters between the migrant workers and the bus driver, and the emphasis of the internet messages on the social order and the moral values that sustain the orderly modern urban world. The debate entries cited in the data presentation, whether they are on the side of the migrant workers or on the side of the bus driver, all illustrate the rigidity and inflexibility of identity categorisation on the public and institutional scale, on which people invoke general social rules of normal and abnormal, and invoke such categorical notions as social class, ethnicity and place of origin. In this example I also want to show that, although people can choose what to wear, how to speak, how to behave, what identity to claim, there is always a limit to this freedom of choice; what people choose is constrained by the unequal and stratified resources available to them. It is probably more revealing to consider why such resources are not available to them – the migrant workers could have chosen taking off their stained work attire before taking the bus, but that tacit norm is not available to them, and their – as well as the bus driver's – choice of discursive and non-discursive activities are conditioned by the general patterns of social inequality on a higher level.

'But that would be wasted'

So far we have looked at identity making discourses produced and circulated in the public sphere; Examples 5.1 and 5.2 show how migrant identities are constructed through conventional public communication media – a periodical article – and a new form of communication media affecting the structure of the public space – the internet – respectively. In what follows, I present an example of institutional discourse and analyse the construction and constraints of the institutional discourses on the migrant identity making. It is an instance of the process mentioned earlier, whereby higher-order categorisations are brought into interactional events and give shape to them. The data are taken from an interview that was carried out in the afternoon of 21 June 2007. The interviewee is Miss Li, the Director of Education, Discipline and Administration (DEDA, *jiaodao zhuren*) of Beili Primary School. DEDA is a managerial position in Chinese primary and secondary schools. A DEDA usually has no teaching duty, but is in charge of administrative affairs and student moral issues. DEDA reports directly to the headmaster. Miss Li used to be a Chinese language teacher. As part of her career development, she was appointed to the managerial position a year before my fieldwork in the school. The management role gives her an insight into the school's problems and challenges at an institutional level. The interview is about 'the merit student award' (*sanhao xuesheng*, literally 'three-good student'), a national award system for primary and secondary school students. The winners of the merit student award have to be outstanding in all three aspects of academic performance, morality and physical and mental fitness. The system works at several levels. From the elementary level of the class wide, to the school wide, district wide, city wide, province wide and up to the nation wide. At the most elementary level of the class-wide and sometimes school-wide election, pupils vote for merit students of their own classes or schools. For the higher levels, school recommendations are essential for a candidate to become a winner. As Miss Li points out in the interview, those who are merit students for the final three years (Grades 4, 5 and 6) of their primary education are recommended candidates by the school for the appraisal at the district and city levels. The interview takes place in the staff office, which is shared by seven teachers, and as the interview proceeds, a teacher, Miss Zhao, whose desk is next to that of Miss Li joins us (line 50) and gives her opinion on the topic.

Example 5.3: '... but that would be wasted ...'

1   Miss Li: ... if the local pupils and the migrant pupils are similar, we could still hope (for local pupils to be elected as merit students). But they are too different.
    JD: You are talking about 'similar' and 'different', what do you mean by being
5   'similar' and 'different'? Do you mean their performance?
    Miss Li: Yes, performance. (For example) in Grade 3 the migrant pupils are very good and the local pupils are mostly underachieving, they were to elect four school wide merit students, the result of the election was that three were migrant pupils and only one was a local. They (the local pupils) are not as
10 good and we couldn't do anything. Then the merit students are mostly migrant pupils, but that (their awards) is not useful.
    JD: Did you mean by 'useful', for example, in their entering a middle school?
    Miss Li: Yes, in finding themselves a good middle school, holding a merit student award is an advantage for a local pupil in searching for good middle
15 school.
    JD: How does it work (for middle school entrance)?
    Miss Li: (It is useful if one is the merit student of a) successive three-year: Grades 4, 5 and 6.
    JD: hmm ...

20 **Miss Li:** There is nothing we could do. We only have more and more migrant pupils. There are about 20 pupils in one class and only five or six (of them) are local, we could hardly find qualified local candidates for the merit students award.
JD: hmm
25 **Miss Li:** It happens that the merit student award is <u>wasted</u>; such as in a nearby school, there is no city-wide merit student candidate this year, I asked why, they said that there used to be two (candidates for the city-wide merit student award), one is a migrant pupil, the other is local. The Beijing local pupil moved to another school. The merit student award is <u>not useful</u> for a migrant
30 pupil.
JD: hmm
Miss Li: They <u>gave up</u> the appraisal for the city-wide merit student award, they could send one candidate, but they had <u>no one</u> to send.
JD: But why?
35 **Miss Li:** The candidate must be district-wide merit student for all three academic years of Grades 4, 5 and 6.
JD: Couldn't the migrant pupil compete for city-wide merit student?
Miss Li: *They could compete, but that would be a waste of opportunity after all* ... no matter how good he (a migrant pupil) is, he will end up with Jian
40 Qiang middle school, or if his parents are rich, they could pay high tuition for a good middle school, then he <u>does not need that</u> (merit student award) at all.
JD: If a Beijing pupil, if he has that (merit student award), he could go to a good middle school?
Miss Li: It is at least an advantage. For example, if a high tuition fee is
45 requested, he (or his parents) could ask for a discount.
JD: Then for migrant pupils, even if he has it ...
Miss Li: They (middle school) <u>don't accept</u> (migrant pupils) at all. All migrant pupils (of this district) are put into one middle school.
JD: No matter how good he is ...
50 **Miss Zhao:** Currently it (local pupils' tuition fees) is <u>all paid by the district government</u>, the money of the district is for the <u>children of the district</u>. Children of He Bei (province), Zhe Jiang (province), they have their own money for their own children. It shouldn't be that they (migrant children) use up the money of <u>Beijing children</u>.
55 **Miss Li:** <u>They (migrant children) come and share our pupils</u>' money.
Miss Zhao: Exactly.
Miss Li: For example, if a Beijing child gets a subsidy of 80 RMB, and if we have five Beijing pupils, then we get 400 RMB (from the government), <u>but the problem is that the money has to pay for many migrant children's schooling</u> ...

(Fieldwork recording, 2007-06-21-V049)

Analysis and interpretation

The content of the interview can be paraphrased and interpreted as follows. Miss Li starts the topic by stressing the difference between the migrant pupils and the local pupils of her school (lines 1–3); she goes on to explain what she means by 'too different' through an example of the Grade 3 class – the migrant pupils of that class (pupils aged about nine or 10) are satisfactory in their performance, whereas the local Beijing pupils are almost all underachieving. In their election of the merit students of the class, three out of the four merit students are migrant pupils. Winning the merit student award is 'not useful', however, for the migrant students (line 11). I ask Miss Li to elaborate what she means by 'useful'. According to her, the usefulness of the merit student award lies in enhancing local Beijing pupils' chance of being admitted to a top middle school (lines 14–16). Miss Li explains that it would be an 'advantage' for a local Beijing pupil – a pupil of Beijing *hukou*-holder – in hunting for a good middle school if he or she is a merit student, especially a merit student of the final three successive years (Grades 4, 5 and 6) of their primary schooling (lines 18–19).

Miss Li indicates that there is nothing the school could do to change the situation. The situation is that the Beili neighbourhood sees an influx of migrant families and the school is increasingly populated with migrant pupils. It is a small school (about 150 pupils), and at the time of fieldwork merely one-fourth of the pupils are local. Within such a small pool of local students, the school finds it hard to 'find qualified local candidates for the merit students award' (lines 23 and 24). This is also what Miss Li means by 'we could still hope' in lines 1 and 2 – the school could still hope for more local pupils to be elected as merit students if the local and the migrant pupils are comparable in performance –, and by 'we couldn't do anything' in line 10 – the migrant pupils outperform the local and the teachers could not do anything to have more local pupils voted to be merit students.

Miss Li is well informed of similar situations faced by other schools, due to her position as DEDA. She gives an example of a nearby primary school. Its opportunity of recommending a qualified candidate for the city-wide merit student award appraisal is 'wasted' (line 26), because the local candidate moves to another, probably a more prestigious, school and automatically gives up the appraisal. 'The merit student award is <u>not useful</u> for a migrant pupil,' Miss Li repeats and stresses in line 30. The school gives up the opportunity, she continues; they have a chance to recommend one pupil out of the two candidates, but the local candidate moves elsewhere and the school is left with no candidate. This explanation does not include the possibility of recommending the migrant candidate for the appraisal; I therefore ask for further elaboration. Miss Li's answer '[t]hey could compete, but that would be a waste of opportunity after all' (lines 38 and 39) is in a weaker voice than the rest of her utterance, which probably signals her hesitation in giving the opinion. According to Miss Li, whether the migrant candidate enters the city-wide appraisal or not, and whether he or she would win or not, the opportunity would be 'wasted', because the award would not be an advantage for a migrant pupil in being admitted by a prestige Beijing middle school. She explains that no matter what award a migrant pupil holds, the middle school she or he could normally end up with was Jian Qiang School, an underachieving middle school that receives a special subsidy from the district government for admitting migrant pupils of the district, unless their parents could purchase them a place in a prestigious middle school taking big fees, in which case neither performance nor award record would be relevant, as Miss Li indicates (lines 39–41).

I ask Miss Li for an explicit comparison between the 'usefulness' of the merit student award for migrant pupils and that for local pupils. Her explanation reiterates what she says earlier in the interview – the award is an advantage for local pupils and is of no use for migrant pupils as local middle schools simply 'don't accept (migrant pupils) at all' (line 47). Miss Zhao, a Chinese language teacher who has been around for a while and must have heard part of our conversations, interrupts us (line 50) and gives her opinion. Her move of joining the interview might be a result of my comment in line 49 '[n]o matter how good he is …'; it is a repetition of what Miss Li says in line 39, but the disapproval tone of the utterance is 'visible' and may function as a stimulation of Miss Zhao's utterance.

Miss Zhao emphasises that local pupils' costs of education are 'all paid by the district government', and that the amount of district subsidy is for 'the district's children', that is, children of the *hukou*-holders. Migrant pupils have their own shares of government subsidy at their *hukou* locality; according to Miss Zhao, and being non-*hukou* holders in Beijing schools, they 'use up the money of Beijing children'. This argument is agreed upon by Miss Li 'They (migrant children) come and share our pupils' money.' Miss Li gives an example of how the government subsidy works, and stresses that 'but the problem is that money has to pay for many migrant children's schooling' (lines 50–58). In this part of the conversation, both the teacher and the DEDA use emphases frequently, which may suggest that they feel strongly about migrant pupils who miss their home subsidy and have to share that of local Beijing

Scale 3: Institutions

pupils. The school is therefore under financial pressure because it does not receive as much subsidy as would fit to the number of children they educate.

What is striking in this interview is the use of the adjectives 'not useful' and 'wasted' by Miss Li and Miss Zhao – becoming a merit student is 'not useful' for a migrant pupil and the advantage of being a merit student would be 'wasted' if it is granted to a migrant pupil. Both Miss Li and Miss Zhao produced these utterances in the way that it is a mere pragmatic concern to maximise the advantage of the award by having the local pupils, not the migrant, become merit students. I trust that they do not intentionally treat the local and the migrant unequally; they perhaps see the selectiveness of award candidates as simply a pragmatic issue. Miss Li and Miss Zhao are both key informants of mine, and as an ethnographer, I work with them on a daily basis as well as observe their approaches of dealing with their migrant pupils constantly. I can confidently say they are caring, encouraging, responsible, and professional both towards the local pupils and towards the migrant ones. At the linguistic and communicative exchange scale, what I observe are overwhelmingly friendly interactions between the migrant and the local; at the metapragmatic scale it is still rare to pinpoint any differentiation between the two groups. It is only when my gaze moves to the institutional level, that the pattern of inequality and the constraints of the institutional differentiation emerge.

There are two folds of the institutional constraints demonstrated by the interview. First, the discourses of Miss Li and Miss Zhao on the link between the merit student award and the locality of the award holders are determined by the tacit institutional policy, the practical rule that favours local pupils over migrant pupils in selecting award candidates. Miss Li and Miss Zhao seem to believe that it is only natural and practical to favour local pupils, because of how the award system works – it only brings benefits to local award holders, not the migrants; it would make no difference for a migrant pupil's academic career. There is no doubt a practical layer in this argument, but behind this practical layer stands the fact that the merit student awards are not concerned only with 'merits', but that migrant identity plays a considerable role in the performance-based student appraisal.

The second fold of the institutional constraints is the identity categorisations that Miss Li and Miss Zhao make by comparing and contrasting the local and the migrant pupils in the final part of the interview (lines 51–61). In their daily interactions with and their metapragmatic comments on migrant pupils, Miss Li and Miss Zhao perform the duties of a teacher who ought to be supportive and fair. Speaking from an institutional level, however, they classify the migrant and the local pupils into two rigid and static groups that are not only defined by the administrative notions, but also contrasted in the distribution of educational resources. Their discourses are echoed by what the vice headmaster once describes to me about a headmasters' meeting at the district educational authority, during which a participant says 'don't let our district educate migrant pupils of the entire country (note: the district is burdened by its very high percentage of migrant population compared to that of the other Beijing districts)' (Fieldnotes, 2007-05-17). One could argue that migrant children could obtain their fair share of government subsidy if they 'chose' to attend school in their *hukou* locality. This argument, which is circulated frequently among teachers, migrants, as well as in the media, essentially abnormalises migrant children's presence in urban schools – migrant children move into cities and bring 'troubles' to the urban education system which has been devised for local children, not for migrant. Along this line of argument, receiving education back in their hometown would be the 'best' (or 'normal') choice of migrant children, which is what actually many migrant children in my fieldwork opted for eventually; but it appears to me that they do not 'choose' to move back, but are forced by the institutional mechanism of the education system. The merit student award is but one example of the function of such mechanism; more decisive concerns include their chances of a promising middle school education and their eventual opportunity for a college placement. The abnormality underlying the discourse of Miss Li and Miss Zhao, as well as that of the vice headmaster's, is that the influx of migrant children into the neighbourhood disrupts the 'normal' operation of the school and the 'normal' mechanism of educational resource distribution. This perception is determined, not by the speakers' own wish, but by the way the educational system runs, by the institutional inequality as a social construct, and by the wider social pattern and structure.

Summary

Chapter 5 begins by introducing the central notions of 'abnormality', 'stigma', 'normality' and 'modernity'. I use Foucault's notion of 'abnormal' with an emphasis on its essential meaning of 'being deviated from normal', and Goffman's notion of 'stigmatised individual' as the one who falls short of our 'normative expectations' in this chapter. Both notions are essential in the data analysis and interpretation to illustrate the construction and constraints of institutional and public discourses on the making of migrant identity.

The analytical part of this chapter includes three examples. The first example is a periodical article advising potential migrant workers to achieve a good level of Putonghua proficiency before moving to the urban areas. The migrant worker is abnormalised against an image of the ideal urban youth in the conventional media of public discourse, and the migrant identity is strictly defined in comparison and contrast to the Putonghua speaking urban citizen. The second example is concerned with a new form of journalism – the internet, which has largely restructured the public space. The data analysis focuses on a long debate entry combined with textual and visual signs. The migrant workers are abnormalised for their behaviour being deviated from the tacit urban norms, and stigmatised because of their incapability of 'normifying' themselves. For the third example, I include an interview of the Director of Education, Discipline and Administration of Beili School on the meaning of being 'merit student' for the migrant pupils. The interviewees' use of terms such as 'not useful' and 'wasted' catch my attention. The presence of migrant children in the urban education system is collectively abnormalised in the sense that they bring disorder, and hence problems and pressures, to the urban education institution. This example reveals the structural inequality that works against the migrant pupils.

In all three examples we observe that modernity emphasises order; it works against categories such as migrants whose identity features are easily seen as disruptive of the 'normal' social order. We also observe, in these three examples, people invoke general social norms and administrative notions when producing discourses from the public and institutional scale, and the identity categories are no longer flexible and fluid, such as those instantiated in Chapters 3 and 4, but are rigid, static and general. Identities of the three scales penetrate, collaborate and interact with each other, and these interactions will be addressed in the next chapter.

Notes

1. The table of contents of this periodical is available at: http://www.cqvip.com/qk/86404X/200501/index.html. Last accessed on 15.7.09.
2. Relevant regulations and policies can be found at the official website of the National Language and Literacy Working Committee (NLLWC): http://www.china-language.gov.cn. Last accessed on 15.7.09. The NLLWC is part of China Ministry of Education.

3. The online forum is available at: http://dzh2.mop.com/mainFrame.jsp?url=http://dzh2.mop.com/topic/readQues_9013555_0_0.html. Last accessed on 15.7.09.
4. The situation is improving though; see http://news.xinhuanet.com/politics/2009-02/08/content_10782192.htm for recent change in migrant workers' social welfare issue. Last accessed on 15.7.09.

Chapter 6
Conclusions and Reflections

Back to the Coca-Cola Can

This book begins with a proposal of a three-scale framework to study the migrant identity construction in urban Beijing. In the introductory chapter, I explain why we need such a framework and what the framework is about. In doing so, I review and evaluate recent identity studies, particularly, CA and CDA, and argue that although being important for the present study, both CA and CDA approaches are insufficient in addressing the discursive processes of identity making in the complex and stratified social reality.

What differentiates the three-scale approach from CA and CDA? This question can be answered by a re-use of the Coca-Cola can metaphor from a slightly different angle (see Figure 6.1a–c).

Figure 6.1a is a view saturated with a tiny part of the Coca-Cola can; it is the view we could obtain if we observe the can so closely that we only see a very small part of it in great details, but lose sight of the rest. Taking some distance, we get the view of Figure 6.1b – a whole picture of the can, but only of the can; observing it from farther away, as Figure 6.1c shows, we could see the can right next to other objects such as a mobile phone, a pen, and the table on which it stands. Figure 6.1a resembles CA which focuses on small details of language use and identity making, but loses sights of bigger views; Figure 6.1b can be a metaphor of CDA that emphasises the imposition of the contexts on the identity formation but restricts the analysis to just discourse. The three-scale framework I propose here, in contrast, is a broader approach in that it synthesises the basic assumptions of CA, CDA, together with other layers of discursive practice into a scalar structure, so as to offer a more comprehensive understanding of identity making processes and to avoid traps of reductionism and essentialism in identity studies. Emerged out of my fieldwork observations of the discrepancies between CA/CDA and the actual social practice, the

Figure 6.1 (a) Detailed view, (b) front view and (c) distance view of a Coca-Cola can

three-scale framework is designed to capture and to deal with the essentially stratified nature of society. To recap briefly, the three scales are:

(1) The linguistic and communicative exchange scale, on which linguistic interactions occur, and small features of language use, such as accents, index a dialogical process of identity making in the social space (the communicative scale).
(2) The metapragmatic discourse scale, on which identities are commented, evaluated, ratified, by oneself and by others through metapragmatic discourses (the metapragmatic scale).
(3) The public and institutional discourse scale, on which identity building discourses are circulated in the public sphere, identities are defined in rigid bureaucratic and administrative categorisations, and people's general evaluative remarks invoke social norms and rules of social conducts (the public scale).

Chapter 1 spells out the objectives of my research: (1) to understand the making of migrant identities on different scales, and (2) to gain an insight into the transitional Chinese society and social structure (re-)formation through language use and identity making of migrant workers and their children. It also lists the basic assumptions of identity and identity construction: (1) identities are established in social practice; (2) identities are multiple and stratified in relation to the unequally distributed identity building resources; and (3) identities are achieved as well as ascribed.

Chapter 2 outlines the social and methodological backgrounds of the study. The chapter is divided into two parts. The first part deals with the social contexts of China's mass rural–urban migration, the sociolinguistic contexts of the diversified and complex linguistic landscape of the country and the institutional contexts of the education provision to migrant children. The second part gives an account of the ethnographic approach that has guided my research. It argues that the ethnographic approach situates language deeply in social life and this gives a particular strength to the data collection instruments employed within this approach in researching identity construction, a discursive process precisely about the relationship between language and society.

Chapters 3, 4 and 5 report on migrant identity construction at the three scales, respectively. All three chapters follow a similar structure. First, they introduce the notions that are central to each chapter: space, sociolinguistic scale and monoglot language ideology for Chapter 3, ethnolinguistic identity and speech community for Chapter 4, abnormality, stigma and modernity for Chapter 5. Put together, these central notions form a theoretical toolkit for the data analysis and interpretation in this book. All three chapters subsequently present and analyse key episodes and extracts selected from the fieldwork data. Chapter 3 presents three examples of migrant identity construction on the scale of linguistic and communicative exchanges. Example 3.1 is a story told by a Sichuan migrant child who attends an urban public primary school. The story is about the experiences of her first school day, and particularly about her use of dialect while introducing herself to the class, which causes laughter from her fellow-pupils. Example 3.2 is about a migrant worker – a cleaner of a neighbourhood swimming pool – being silenced by her accent, and her linguistic competence being misrecognised. Example 3.3 is a linguistic interaction between a street vendor and me, in which the street vendor deploys various linguistic patterns and resources, navigates language obstacles and articulates multiple identities accordingly. All three examples demonstrate the fluidity and flexibility of identities constructed on this scale, and the indexical connections between the informants' accents and their identities.

In Chapter 4, there are four examples of metapragmatic discourses evaluating the identities of migrant pupils, either by migrant pupils themselves or by others such as their urban counterparts and their teachers. All four examples are from the fieldwork in one Beijing public primary school. Example 4.1 is about a migrant pupil's comments on the migrant identities of her own and fellow migrant pupils during a drawing class. She notably overlays the migrant–local identity contrast with a homogeneous ethnolinguistic identity. Example 4.2 describes evaluative remarks articulated by a group of migrant pupils, particularly by a Jiangxi pupil, on their home dialects during a class break. Example 4.3 is a local Beijing pupil's comments on his migrant classmate's language, identity and performance, and Example 4.4 is a teacher's appraisal on a migrant pupil's language, identity and performance. The four examples instantiate how metapragmatic discourses make identity construction explicit in which people produce identity evaluations, and categorise themselves as well as others into social categories. Identities claimed by oneself at the linguistic and communicative scale are ratified, negotiated, imposed or challenged by others at the metapragmatic scale.

Chapter 5 comprises three examples of identity making discourses produced and circulated on the public and institutional scale. Example 5.1 is a periodical article urging potential migrant worker to learn Putonghua before moving to cities. Example 5.2 details internet discussions on a recent news report of a row between an urban bus driver and several migrant workers because the former one require the latter ones to change clothes before taking the bus. Example 5.3 discusses a school staff's naturalisation of an unequal appraisal practice and the education system in general that is discriminatory against migrant pupils. The three examples together illustrate the abnormalisation and stigmatisation of the urban others – the migrants – who introduce disorder to the social norms in the modern urban space.

I use the term 'migrants' throughout the book. 'Migrants', however, is not really *a priori*, but *a posteriori*, in the sense that identity making is a performative process, but very often it is subject to official constraints and institutional discourses. For example, a judge declares someone a criminal, and from that moment on, he is a criminal, whether he likes it or not. In the same way, the people that I investigate in this book are *migrants*, perhaps not so much on the lower level of everyday interaction (where identities can be fluid and flexible), but on the highest level of institutional discourses. Therefore, my critiques of constructionism is that modern society is organised on the basis of clear categories and these categories are real. These categories are the framework within which most social life is organised. For instance, elit migrants – those who immigrate to Beijing as middle-class 'white collar workers' – are non-stereotypical migrants but they share the same constraints as lower working class migrant workers in many ways, such as having difficulties in sending their children to local public schools. Therefore, they do not correspond to the stereotype of migrants, but even these big social economic differences are grounded in the same institutional constraints.

In short, this book has structured a theoretical framework of researching discursive processes of identity construction, and reports on an ethnographic fieldwork to demonstrate this framework. It fulfills the first objective of my research, that is, to study migrant identity making at three scales. This conclusive chapter is organised around the theoretical, empirical and methodological reflections of the research through a second look at some of the data presented in the previous chapters. In doing so, I move to consider the fast-changing Chinese society and social structure (re-)formation, an insight gained from my fieldwork observation of migrant workers as an emerging social stratum. This will fulfil the second objective of the book.

Theoretical Reflections

The argument I build in this book revolves around an image of social reality as scalar, as structured into different scales. There can be unlimited number of scales but I choose the three scales to demonstrate that one scale is inadequate in analysing complex social phenomena such as identity construction. Moreover, each of these scales is the focus of a tradition of identity research, and each of them represents only a partial view of identity. By distinguishing them as scales of a layered process, we arrive at a more comprehensive image of identity. Consequently, each scale has features of its own: there are rules and conventions that operate at the different scale-levels, and these rules and conventions make certain things possible and others impossible. A multifaceted analysis of social phenomena requires attention to the various scales and their features; not paying attention to the scalar nature of social phenomena would risk homogenising social phenomena in a reductionist move which assumes that a single set of rules and conventions dominate them. Given that ethnography has as its traditional ambition to be comprehensive in description and analysis, my ethnographic study tries to be just that by attending to the different scales at which we see social phenomena being played out.

Having said that, and reiterating what I said at the outset, we must of course be aware that the three scale-levels I identify in this book also operate together in one spatiotemporally bound event. We can observe social phenomena only in their synchronic deployment, while we must realise that what we see is 'synchronised' (Blommaert, 2005a), that it is an interplay of features from different scale-levels in one situated event. To be more specific, identity is a scalar, layered and non-unified phenomenon. In actual social events, the different scales collapse into one sequence of observable practices (a synchronised observable practice). We should not be led to believe that only the observable practices count, however. The various scales do play a role, they organise and create different processes that constitute a phenomenon for which we have just one name: identity.

Social phenomena appear as bound, unique and relatively simple, while they hide various layers whose interplay produces the social event as we observe it. This duality, between an observational level of social phenomena (in which these phenomena appear as bound, unique and simple) and an analytical one (in which they appear as layered, structured into scale-levels) is the core of my methodological argument.

The three-scale framework is the structuring element of the analytical part of this book. Each analytical chapter addresses a scale-level by presenting and analysing data from the ethnographic fieldwork. At the end of this book, I bring the three scales together and demonstrate that, instead of being separated, distinct processes, they are different dimensions of one social reality, different perspectives of one observation, different aspects of one identity building process. I shall formulate this argument in two steps: first, identities made on the three scales overlap, interact with and are connected to each other, and the nexus point is indexicality; second, they are of one 'synchronised' social reality perceived from a language ideology level.

In what follows, I deal with the interactions between different scales through a further analysis of the examples from Chapters 3, 4 and 5. I discuss (1) the interactions between the communicative scale and the metapragmatic scale through a re-analysis of Examples 3.3 and 4.3, (2) the interactions between the communicative scale and the public scale through Examples 3.1 and 5.2, and (3) the interactions between the metapragmatic scale and the public scale through Examples 4.1 and 5.3, respectively.

Interactions between the communicative scale and the metapragmatic scale

The interactions between the communicative scale and the metapragmatic scale can be demonstrated by a second look at the street vendor example (Example 3.3). In this case, Xiao Xu creatively deploys his repertoire of linguistic resources in relation to the sociolinguistic spaces of the conversations, and systematically shifts accents, which indexes the shifts of his identity claims. Recall that he speaks with a near-Beijing local accent at the beginning of the commercial talk between him and me – his local customer – which signals his identity of being a Beijing suburban breakfast seller; he shifts to a slightly southern accent while talking about his home town, which indexes a migrant identity; he then shifts to Putonghua and claims identities of being well educated, highly mobile, successfully relocated and quasi-local. This brief outline of the indexical links between his accent shifts and identity claims demonstrates the situatedness and fluidity of the identities performed on the linguistic and communicative scale. In this less-than-three-minute episode of linguistic interaction, however, we can find a subsection of metapragmatic discourse in which, first, both the interlocutors comment on Xiao Xu's Putonghua 'your Putonghua is really good' (lines 15–19), and then Xiao Xu evaluates the accents of other migrants who 'talk in their dialects' (lines 31–36). Note in line 31 my question is 'Do you understand what people speak here in Beijing'; what I intend to find out is his comments on the Beijing accents, on whether Beijing accents are fast or slow, loud or quiet, clear or unclear and so on. Instead of evaluating the Beijing accents, Xiao Xu starts talking about migrant people who speak dialects in Beijing. This misunderstanding of my question implies that the Beijing accents are the default language of the space. Because Putonghua is similar to and is often equalled with the Beijing dialects, it is not a question whether one understands the Beijing accents or not – everyone who enters this space *should* understand it. This misunderstanding points to the hegemonic domination of Putonghua and its devaluing of dialects. The flow of conversations leads the two interlocutors to articulate evaluative remarks that overlap with the identity discussion on the metapragmatic scale.

Furthermore, the self-claimed identities of both interlocutors have to be ratified on the metapragmatic scale. In the transcribed episode, Xiao Xu reverses the question–answer sequence and raises an explicit identity enquiry to me, and I have to subsequently defend my local identity both by an explicit metapragmatic discourse 'I am from here,' and by a stress on the Beijing accent instead of my usual language choice of Putonghua. If we look beyond the interaction event, for example, if we treat the discussions of the street vendor example in this book as a metapragmatic discourse, it becomes clear that the breakfast seller's identities have a longer 'life' than the here-and-now interaction. Although Xiao Xu claims a near-local identity in the encounters, and although I do not challenge this identity claim on the spot, this self-claimed identity is evaluated throughout my analysis, and in a sense denied, as I basically classify him as one of the migrant workers on whom this book is written. His near-local identity, together with my metapragmatic comments in the analysis, will be continuously evaluated by the reader of this book.

The interplays between the two scales do not stop here. They are not confined to the observation that the linguistic and communicative scale is conditioned by the metapragmatic scale. Local language features and linguistic exchanges also index identity making on the metapragmatic scale. For instance, in Example 4.3, Jun produces a metapragmatic discourse on Xing's language use and identities. Jun's marked Beijing accent, in the meantime, brings the linguistic and communicative scale into meta-level identity construction and plays an important role in justifying his position of evaluating his migrant classmate's language. I have used the term a 'Beijing accent' in various places of this book; I now have the opportunity to problematise this term. Beijing accents have several varieties, of which subtle differences often index the speaker's social class, place of origin and sometimes family history. These indexical values have to do with the recent history (of at least 150 years) of Beijing and the demographic makeup of its population. To put it very briefly, the lower and working class has a more remarkable accent than the middle and upper class; inhabitants of the central Beijing city, particularly those who live in the small lanes (*hutong*) of central Beijing city such as the neighbourhood of Beili School described in Chapter 4, have a 'purer' Beijing accent than people from the suburban districts, and the accents of suburban Beijing people are sometimes hybrids of Beijing Mandarin and the dialects of its nearby Hebei province; people whose family have been Beijing inhabitants for generations (*lao Beijing*, literally 'old-Beijing' people) have a more marked central Beijing accent than the immigrants of the latest 60 years.

Jun's accent, to my ear, is that of working class and of central Beijing inhabitants; it may also suggest that he is from a family of Beijing inhabitants for generations. Whereas it is now impossible for me to check the last point, it is confirmed by his teacher that Jun is from a working class family of the neighbourhood. Throughout the interview, Jun's linguistic features, a marked Beijing accent, index a local identity, which in turn guarantees his 'authority', together with his explicitly claimed local identity, in judging Xing's language and identity. Example 4.3 is primarily a metapragmatic discourse produced by Jun on the language and identity of his migrant classmate; his linguistic features, however, index the social factors that are crucial for the identity making in the evaluative remarks. Here, we observe that elements of the linguistic and communicative scale enter the metapragmatic scale and have an impact on the identity construction of the latter one.

Interactions between the communicative scale and the public scale

The two cases we have looked at so far illustrate the interactions between the communicative and the metapragmatic scales. The communicative scale further interacts with the public scale. Rigid and general identity categorisations on the higher scale, that is, on the public and institutional scale, often constrain identity making on the lower, that is, communicative scale, and the flexibility of identity claims at the communicative scale tend to disappear in the public scale. Take the Sichuan child case of Chapter 3, for example. The Sichuan child starts her urban primary schooling with a marked Sichuan accent which labels her as a migrant child, and she ends the narration by being content with her Putonghua proficiency and with her newly achieved urban identity. Seeing from the public and institutional scale, the Sichuan child's story, which is also a public discourse – a newspaper article, invokes a general social rule that distinguished the 'good' social behaviour, the behaviour that fits into the social order, for example, speak Putonghua, from the 'bad' behaviour, the behaviour that breaks the social norms, for example, speak with an accent in school. A second looking at this example from the public scale, we can say that the flexibility of the Sichuan child's identity construction on the lower scale is constrained by general rules of social conducts, and her changing identity claims are replaced by rigid and static administrative notions of identity categorisation. In other words, as soon as our gaze moves upward to the public and institutional discourse scale, the fluid and ever-changing identities that people perform, enact and claim in relation to their linguistic features at the lower linguistic and communicative scale are replaced by an abstract social normality, and by general identity classifications of urban vs. migrant, standard Putonghua vs. vernacular and so on.

On the other side of the interaction, the linguistic features at the lower linguistic scale also index the discursive identity making on the public and institutional scale. Such an example can be found in the 'Changing clothes' case of Example 5.2. This case describes a social encounter between seven migrant workers and an urban bus driver, illustrating the public discourses on the general social norms and rules that demarcate the normal orderly social behaviour from the 'abnormal' behaviour, and demarcate normal urban identity from 'abnormal' migrant identity. This case has a dimension of the linguistic and communicative scale – the linguistic exchanges between the migrant workers and the bus driver (on whose side a few passengers). The news report does not describe the language spoken by the bus driver, or that of the migrant workers, but the internet debate itself is a communicative and interactional event. The news report mentions the content of the exchanges between the urban bus driver and the migrant workers – the bus driver requires the migrant workers to change clothes, the migrant workers refuse, and subsequently phone the bus operation company to raise a complaint. The news report also describes the encounter as a 'row' which gives us an image of how the language exchanges are like – a probably minor verbal conflict with such details as raising voices and using provocative words.

Interactions between the metapragmatic scale and the public scale

We have seen the interactions between the communicative and the metapragmatic scales, and between the communicative and public scales; let us now turn to the interactions between the metapragmatic and the public scales. In the drawing class example (Example 4.1), the pupil who drew me articulates a clear identity discourse, which overlays the distinction between the urban and the migrant identities with a national identity, or, a homogeneous ethnolinguistic identity. As I show in the analysis of this example in Chapter 4, the two identity categories, a migrant identity and a national ethnolinguistic identity, are neither contradictory nor exclusive to each other. Rather, they function in different dimensions – the dimension of rural–urban migration and the dimension of collective membership of an ethnolinguistic community. Here I would like to argue that from the perspective of the three-scale theoretical framework, the pupil's claim of an ethnolinguistic identity involves general social norms on the public and institutional scale: the norms that pupils should avoid explicitly talking about the social distance between the rich and the poor, the urban and the rural, the higher and the lower classes, but stress on the egalitarian notion of all being Chinese. The pupil's discourse can be seen as a jump across scales from a metapragmatic evaluation of her own and her fellow-pupil's identities to a general public and administrative discourse that invokes the 'one language, one culture, one nation' ideology, which sticks a static and abstract identity label – the ethnolinguistic identity – to her and her classmate. When people articulate identity making discourses in a general way, using categories such as native vs. immigrant, or urban vs. rural, the categorisations become rigid and abstract. In this drawing class example, we observe the emergence of a stable ethnolinguistic identity out of the public and institutional scale that intertwines with the identities claimed and negotiated on the metapragmatic scale. It demonstrates the involvement of the public scale in the identity making on the metapragmatic scale.

A final example shows the impacts of the metapragmatic scale on the identity making of the public and institutional scale. Example 5.3 is an institutional discourse that reveals the structural inequality working against the migrant pupils from a higher scale. On this scale, we see the rigidly defined administrative identity categorisations disqualify migrant pupils from being awarded as a 'merit student' on an equal basis. This discourse, meanwhile, is also a metapragmatic evaluation of a school staff on the pupils' identities and performance. In these evaluative remarks, the migrant pupils are contrasted with the local pupils in terms of their academic performance, the outlook of their academic career, and their chances of being awarded with 'merit students'. These contrasts are based on a taken-for-granted administrative identity categorisation defined in the migrant pupils' *hukou* record and in the institutional discourse of school registry. The content of this interview is the administratively defined identity categorisation, but here we see that this content is wrapped in the form of metapragmatic discourse, which is again conditioned by the public and institutional scale.

In short, the three scales interact in complex and multiple ways; they are connected with each other through indexicality in the sense that small linguistic features point to and invoke 'bigger' social meanings and processes. The re-analysis and re-interpretation of the examples from Chapters 3, 4 and 5 has revealed the connections, interaction, and co-development of identities on different scales. In what follows I argue that the scales are varying dimensions of one social reality if we look at them from a language ideology perspective.

A language ideological perspective

The term 'language ideology' appears frequently in this book; in Chapter 1, I argue that the political and ideological contexts are often privileged in identity studies that follow a CDA approach. Chapter 2 describes the rise of Putonghua as the centre of a monoglot language ideology. In Chapter 3, 'monoglot language ideology' is one of the key concepts. Throughout the three examples of Chapter 3, we see the work of a monoglot ideology that values Putongua as the 'correct' language and misrecognises the non-standard linguistic resources and practice on the linguistic and communicative scale. In Chapter 4, the central notion of 'speech community' is conceptualised within the language ideology tradition. The notion of 'monoglot ideology' is again a key theoretical tool in this chapter. All four examples of Chapter 4 are from a school – a state institution that is dominated by and meanwhile reproduces such language ideologies. On the metapragmatic scale, we observe that the informants explicitly articulate a monoglot language ideology through metapragmatic comments, evaluations and activities. In Chapter 5, the public and institutional discourses function in producing and circulating the dominant language ideology on a massive scale. We can trace the ideological constraints in each example. In the periodical article, potential migrant workers are urged to learn Putonghua prior to their migration to fit the urban social order; in the internet discussions on whether migrant workers should follow the urban norms, the migrant workers encounter urban mainstream ideologies of social conducts, whereas the conceptions and practices of the migrant workers are marginalised; and in the interview of the DEDA on the inequality of the urban schooling system, the interviewee's taken-for-granted position of the unequal awarding mechanism appears under the mask of being practical in making the most of the awards. All three examples are telling in terms of the production and reproduction of the dominant ideologies.

In this concluding chapter, I discuss what language ideology means for the three-scale structure identity making of my study. Rather than an extensive discussion on language ideology (interested readers are referred to Blommaert, 2006b; Silverstein, 1998), I briefly trace the scholarly evolvement of language ideology, state my position in the understanding of this notion, and argue for its presence in the theorisation of the three-scale framework.

The conceptualisation of ideology evolves along two visible strands: the Marxist tradition of class-bound ideology and the Durkheimian tradition of neutrally defined underlying layers that classify people into communities, cultures and societies. Linguistics comes relatively late in the ideology debates. A notable exception is Silverstein's work on indexicality and ideology (Silverstein, 1979, 1981, 1996), which grows out of the domain of linguistic anthropology. The notion of indexicality is the key for conceptualising language ideology. In his early work on language ideology, Silverstein defines language ideology as 'sets of beliefs about language articulated by users as a rationalization of justification of perceived language structure and use' (Silverstein, 1979: 193). This definition suggests, however, that the language user explicitly articulates language ideology (which is subsequently complemented by his work on 'the limits of awareness'; Silverstein, 1981). The understanding of language ideology remains somewhat vague in Schieffelin et al. (1998), a book that brings language ideology to the front of scholarly debates. In Kroskrity (2000), a landmark book following closely on the previous one, we get a clearer picture of this concept. Kroskrity (2000) argues that language ideologies are perceptions of language in the interest of a specific social group, that they are multiple due to the multiplicity of meaningful social divisions, that people have various levels of awareness of language ideologies, and that they bridge language users' linguistic resources and their sociocultural experience.

Following this tradition and sharing its basic preoccupations, I argue that, first, language ideologies are more often than not taken for granted by language users, and typically appear in the forms of tacit rules of social and linguistic practices. A remarkable work of language ideologies is naturalising the hegemonic domination of one language or language variety as the 'correct' linguistic form, against which other languages or language varieties are measured and evaluated. Second, and related to the first point, language ideologies are the ideologies of the dominant social groups; language ideologies of subordinate groups are by definition non-ideological, because ideologies are always tools and properties of the dominant social groups and are always directly connected to maintaining such domination. Although often being portrayed as the 'universal truth', language ideologies notably 'distort' the social reality through the lens of the dominant social groups. Third, language ideologies are articulated and circulated at various scale levels, and we have seen examples of that in the preceding chapters.

In the remaining part of this section, I illustrate these understandings of language ideology through a re-analysing Example 4.2, and argue that the three identity making scales are different dimensions of one social reality, perceived from a language ideology angle. Recall the episode that happened in the Grade 4 classroom during a class break. I ask the pupils to show me their home dialects. A Jiangxi pupil hesitates to speak in her dialect, and comments that it sounds 'terrible', 'not good', 'like a foreign language'; a Zhejiang child says that she was born and grows up in Beijing and 'of course' she speaks Putonghua; a Henan pupil says that she speaks dialect with her parents at home; a boy refers me to a Beijing pupil for dialect knowledge. It is primarily a metapragmatic discourse in which the migrant pupils evaluate their home dialects and comment on their language choice in different social settings. On this metapragmatic scale, we can see the work of monoglot language ideology in the migrant pupils' evaluative remarks, which ridicules and abnormalises their home dialects.

This episode is, at the same time, a social encounter between the migrant pupils and me, seen from the linguistic and communicative scale. We can detect such linguistic features and styles from the fieldnotes as 'with a prolonged and emphasised "nothing" indicating reluctance and shyness' when the Jiangxi pupil explains why she does not want to show me her dialect; 'laughter from the children' triggered by the Jiangxi pupil's utterance; the Jiangxi pupil 'said something in her dialect, laughing' at herself. From these style descriptions, we can see that the Jiangxi pupil is ashamed of her dialect, which triggers laughter both from her fellow-pupils and from herself. The shyness, the hesitation, the laughter, all point to the same ideological process with that of the metapragmatic scale: the dialect is measured against Putonghua and is disqualified. This language ideology is internalised and inscribed in the pupils' linguistic habitus through such linguistic and communicative events, and is reproduced in their metapragmatic discourses. The two scales, perceived from this angle, are two facets of one ideological process.

In addition to the Jiangxi pupil's linguistic features and styles, we can distinguish a general shift of the pupils' eagerness in participating the discussion: at the beginning of the conversations, 'they were cheerful and loud, raising their voices and competing with each other for my attention' because they are warm in nature and they are curious, whereas later on 'most of the pupils had left me'. This remarkable attitude shift is telling in that they come to me with a hope of talking about something interesting, such as where I come from, why I sit in their classroom, for how long I will be there; but the topic I raise do not interest them. They may find that talking about their home dialects is a dry and sterile topic, there is little to say, because the language they speak is Putonghua, full stop. They may even find the topic embarrassing, as the dialect triggers laughter, indexes unwanted identities and is out of tune with the dominant monoglot language ideology. The language ideology is like the air people live in but rarely give a thought. The native Beijing people whom I come across and talk to almost unexceptionally report that accents and dialects are acceptable as long as people are able to communicate and understand each other. Beneath this pragmatic view, however, accents are measured, and are related to identities through an ideological process that is mostly unspoken, and in many occasions probably unaware. What is striking to me in this case, and in the examples throughout this book, is the observed phenomenon that migrants, the subordinated groups of the society, almost all accept the dominant hegemony of Putonghua and take the monoglot language ideology for granted. This is perhaps what we see in the first example of Chapter 4 that 'even the most disadvantaged, tend to perceive the world as natural and to find it much more acceptable than one might imagine', because 'habitus' converts the hegemonic ideology into normal thoughts and practices (Bourdieu, 1987: 520).

We have seen that there is a dimension of identity making on the linguistic and communicative scale that functions simultaneously on the same agents with that of the metapragmatic scale; we shall see in the following that the public and institutional scale is also present in this case. The Jiangxi pupil's metapragmatic comments 'it doesn't sound good ... [i]t sounds terrible, it sounds like a foreign language ...' are at the same time a discourse functioning on the public and institutional scale, which are concerned with general social norms of being 'good' vs. being 'bad', 'right' vs. 'wrong', 'native' vs. 'migrant'. As we see in Chapter 5, discourses produced on the public and institutional scale typically reduce the identity making process to rigid categorisation, and complex and subtle identity construction gives way to abstract and straightforward demarcation such as 'we have too many migrants', which demarcates migrants from local residents, or 'that accent sounds funny', which demarcates one language variety – the standard language – from other varieties in the same ideological process with what we have just observed on the communicative and metapragmatic scales. The Jiangxi pupil's public discourse is wrapped in her metapragmatic comments, which triggers rigid categorisation of being a migrant pupil, and invokes the general social norm of speaking Putonghua in school. This public scale discourse forms another facet of the monoglot language ideology, an abstract and demarcating facet.

This brief re-analysis of the Jiangxi pupil case demonstrates the work of all three scales in one case, on the same people, at the same time. It offers evidence for the argument that the three identity making scales are not separated or distinct; rather, they are different facets of one process. The clue that brought us to this insight was the presence of a monoglot language ideology in the identity construction processes of each scale – an ideology that is articulated and circulated on all three scales. The theoretical reflections have been concerned with the essential oneness of the scales in actual social events having been testified in two steps – the scales interact with each other, and the scales are different dimensions of one social reality at a language ideological level. The theoretical findings of the present study lead to new insights into the different ways in which identities are constructed through discursive practices.

Empirical Reflections

To a Western reader, this book may be read in a negative way. It is possible that the stories it tells would be generalised to the whole of China, based on an imagined homogeneity and uniformity of the country. This book is critical, yet it makes no attempt to argue that migrant life is solely concerned with discrimination, that little effort has been made to improve the equality between the local and the migrant, or that accents and dialects of migrants are misrecognised in every social encounter. For ethnographic research such as this, there are issues we can connect to wider contexts, and issues we cannot. I first address those issues that we must connect and compare with those in wider social and geographical contexts, and second, I turn to the factors that force us to be cautious in taking a static and homogeneous view of the present research. In the final part of this section, I argue that identity making is more than a discursive process;

an ethnographer has to observe and to take on board discursive practices as well as non-discursive, behavioural, social, psychological and contextual processes.

The migration I sketch is not an entirely novel phenomenon. Its novelty lies in the potential of witnessing the social changes of China from a planned economy to a market-oriented one, from tightly controlled population movements to free and massive migrations, from an idealistic 'classless' proletarian society[1] to a society divided by various classes and class fractions. The line of research on the Chinese rural–urban migration is far from being exhausted, and the scholarly attention it deserves cannot be matched by the relatively small volume of available research. It is, however, an essentially similar phenomenon with regard to the economic immigrations in the West. In the Western European and North American countries, we witness the cross-border influx of economic labour from less affluent societies, in which language and identity travel across spaces as well as across scales. The complexity of linguistic exchanges brought by population movements is carefully documented in Rampton (2005), an interactional analysis of spontaneous speech among urban youth in the United Kingdom. An example of hegemonic domination is Silverstein's (1996) study on monoglot Standard English in the United States. The discriminatory moments documented in this book, such as being required to change clothes to take a bus, are neither uniquely Chinese, nor worse than elsewhere in the world. They are outcomes of the same processes, that is, population movements within the contexts of globalisation, in which people from different communities, people who speak different languages or language varieties and people who organise their lives in line with different social norms, enter into communicative interactions or other types of social encounters. It is important to remember that differences are rarely neutral; they are quickly converted into inequality. It is safe to say that we live in a world of inequality.

What are the issues we should be cautious about? For researching Chinese rural–urban migration, at least two factors merit some attention: the size of the country, and the speed at which social situations could change. The country is huge in size. Everyone would agree. But what does that mean? It means diversity, it means that one social phenomenon would have a very different look in another part of the country, and it means we cannot easily say 'China is so and so'. The data I analyse here essentially document the situation in Beijing, and they cannot be extrapolated to the whole of China just like that. Throughout this book I argue against an imagined homogeneity in language and society. At a micro-level, this can be instantiated by Example 4.3. In this case, Jun's evaluative comments of

Xing's accent, her identity, and her academic performance may give the reader an impression that Jun is seriously discriminatory; however, as my final remarks in that example show, I also observe (and this is the advantage of ethnographic observation) that he is, on many occasions, friendly and spontaneous to Xing and to his other migrant fellow-pupils in their everyday interactions. At this ground level of observation, and this is not particularly to do with the size of China, an ethnographer is compelled to take a non-uniform approach towards obtaining a balanced understanding of people, which is always complicated, non-black-and-white and non-uniform.

At a macro level, the stories of migrant workers in the urban areas appear in diverse forms. For example, it is reported that three migrant workers are elected to be deputies to the National People's Congress (*quanguo renda daibiao*), the highest legislation institution of the country, and more deputies on the regional level of the People's Congress in 2008,[2] which means that they are policy makers who are able to raise bills and to pass laws that favour migrant workers. Furthermore, the public discourses mostly emphasise the social progresses in protecting migrants' rights and in helping their 'integration' into the urban mainstream society. For instance, the *People's Daily* reports that the All-China Federation of Trade Unions makes 'ten progresses' in protecting migrant workers' rights and interest by March 2008.[3] Another example is that the Chongqing[5] city announces that the first Sunday of every November to be the Migrant Workers' Day, in order to raise the public awareness of migrant workers' contribution to the city, and to express urban citizens' gratitude to the contribution of migrant workers.[4] This book is, however, an attempt to balance this over-optimistic view and to unveil the social inequality which is often invisible in an egalitarian ideology that 'the workers are the most honoured and most proud people (*laodong zui guangrong*)' inherited from the era prior the 1980s economic and social reform in China.

The second factor that we have to take into account is the changes in the pattern of China's rural–urban migration. Migration is not a static phenomenon. Rather, it responds sensitively to national as well as global socioeconomic situations. The major part of my fieldwork was carried out during the economic boom between 2006 and 2008. Since late 2008, we have witnessed a global recession, and a new type of migration has emerged – some 20 million migrant workers who have spent years in cities begin returning to their home villages. The new challenges brought by the recession are to enlarge rural employment for a better intake of redundant labourers and to re-train the returnees for higher employability. This is not to say that what has been researched is of the past, as there are hundreds of millions migrant workers who remain in cities, and as the returnees are ready to 'return' to cities when the socioeconomic situations are improved. But this is a change that cannot be neglected, because it makes the rural–urban migration more complex, because the migrant workers have built a richer linguistic repertoire which will further complicate the linguistic landscapes of their hometown, and because their newly subscribed identities will collectively bring a new look to their villages. This point can be illustrated by a story told by a migrant who works as a nanny in Beijing for three years. What I knew about this informant before this conversation is restricted to some basic information, such as that she is in her forties, she was from the Sichuan province and she has two sons who work as construction workers with their father – her husband – in Chengdu, the provincial capital of Sichuan. By the time of data collection, I knew her as a nanny for about a month. The fragment is recorded in a fieldnote.

Extract 6.1: '... I will return to Beijing whenever I can ...'

> She will quit the job and leave for home by the end of this week. She started talking about her family this evening, and told me that she left home for Beijing, because she found that her husband had an affair in Chengdu and he had lied about it for quite a while. She would have a depression if she had stayed at home after knowing the truth. She decided to leave for Beijing to have a new life. When she just arrived, she had nothing, and could not speak Putonghua, 'I couldn't even speak' she said, but later on she got trained to be a nanny, and now she made more money than her husband did. She rarely went back to her hometown in the last three years, not even for last Chinese New Year. She spent her leisure time with friends who were also nannies, and she liked this lifestyle. But now she had to return, because her oldest son was about to have his wedding in their village, and their house had to be rebuilt after the 5.12 Sichuan Wenchuan earthquake of which the epicentre was not very far from her village. 'I will insist on a divorce', she said, which was something she was afraid of before the migration, 'and I will return to Beijing whenever I can'.

(Fieldnotes, 2009-01-14)

Another reason she does not mention in this episode is the recession, due to which the average wage of domestic workers in Beijing has dropped by one-tenth in January 2009, and by one-fifth in April 2009.[6] In this brief account of a long migration journey, the nanny arrives in Beijing with little command of the local language and limited vocational training. She first manages to acquire the language, Putonghua, which enhances her chance of settling. She then obtains the training and becomes a professional nanny, a relatively well-paid job compared to other types of domestic service work (such as cleaning, cooking, taking care of old people and patients, walking dogs etc.). The success in an upscale geographical and social move opens a door for her to a bigger world and to a freer lifestyle, through which she subscribes a new, urban, and successful migrant identity. When various factors force her to return, to make a 'downscaled' move, she is confident in controlling her own life and in making such decisions as whether the marriage continues and where she spends her life. This confidence comes from her access to the resources of a higher scale: the language, the training, the work experience, the social network she has built in the city. Although she is a migrant worker, a working class woman with a rural *hukou*, she has lifted herself (partially and temporarily) from being a farmer, one of the perhaps lowest social classes in nowadays China. In her account, we see a richer language repertoire, a new identity and an empowered person.

In her return to the home village, both the new language and the new identity play a role in her interactions with family members, fellow villagers and friends. The linguistic competence of speaking Putonghua is not present constantly, but her initial Beijing story of not being able to talk and of managing Putonghua in a short time becomes a drive for the younger generation to learn the standard language that often points to a better education and better life opportunities. There are occasional shifts between the local vernacular and Putonghua, which index the nanny's newly achieved identity of having lived and worked in Beijing. The shifts to Putonghua are seen by some as a mark of urban high life, but it also happens that such shifts trigger disfavour from others who have little access to such a linguistic competence and who have never been away from the local community.

Her identity of successfully emigrating to a metropolis such as Beijing has an impact on the power relations between her and her family members. For one thing, she used to fear that her husband would leave her, but now she insists on a divorce and believes that her life will be better without him. It is irrelevant to foresee whether the marriage could move on; the nanny has gained the power to resist the life that she dislikes because she is financially independent, because she knows her way of escape, because she has acquired a different identity. On the one hand, this new urban identity becomes a source of inspiration for those villagers who have a 'city dream'. On the other hand, the new language, the new identity and the decent income compared to what she could make from tilling the fields introduce interruption to the local social order and norms of social conducts, and make her 'abnormal' in a rural social context. It takes the nanny time and efforts to fit back into the rural society that she comes from, she discovers that familiar phenomena become strange and unnatural, and she finds herself to be a stranger at home, someone from elsewhere. In short, she acquires an identity 'in between': in Beijing she is a migrant worker from Sichuan, whereas in her home village she again becomes an outsider, a person of other place.

There is little chance that she will work in the fields as a farmer again when she returns home. It is reported that less than 2.5% migrant returnees resume farming.[7] She will most probably return to Beijing or go to other cities for employment, as it is reported that 90% of the returned migrant workers have left for cities again by April 2009. To what degree the new language and identity of the nanny become involved in her linguistic exchanges and social encounters with her fellow villagers needs further investigation; but she certainly has changed, the urban experience has become part of her *habitus* and travels downscale with her to the village. In these downscaling processes, the nanny's languages and identities are not static entities; rather, the bigger patterns of migration between rural and urban China at a macro level are collapsed in the individual case at the ground level.

So far, we have established connections between China's rural–urban migration and the cross-boarder immigrations in the Western European and North American contexts. Moreover, this section has warned against the possible mis-reading of my study by stressing the diversity of the country and the dynamics of the migration. Next, I position the making of migrant identities within the dimension of social class formation, and argue that identity making is more than a discursive process. In doing so, this chapter fulfils the second aim of the research, that is, to understand the transitional Chinese society and social structure (re-)formation.

Throughout the examples of the three analytical chapters, we can distinguish the mark of lower social class on most informants – the Sichuan child who is laughed at, the street vendor who has to stay outdoor all whole day, the rural hairstyle in the conversations of the two migrant pupils during a drawing class, the way the rural couple dress in the cartoon and so on. Social class is a contested concept in China. The established view is that the state was born out of a proletarian revolution in the first half of the 20th century, in which the proletariat seized the public power and founded the nation on the basis of the scientific socialism ideal of the Marxist tradition. During the 30 years or so planned economy era (more or less between 1949 and 1979), the class structure was rather neatly defined: a peasant class and an industrial working class that included a class fraction of intellectuals. Both classes were of the proletariat, and the means of production was turned into state property. The economic and social reform of the 1980s has posed theoretical as well as practical challenges to this class categorisation. Theoretically, a social group which emerges out of privatisation and which thus has the control over the capital and over the means of production can hardly fit into either class. Practically, we have witnessed reshuffles of classes and class fractions at least in three respects. First, the rapidly polarised distribution of social wealth has given birth to such groups as 'new rich', 'middle class', 'petit bourgeoisie' (*xiaozi*); second, the glory of the working class who used to be emblematic of the advanced and revolutionary social force has gradually faded out, and in this process being an urban industrial worker is downscaled from a prestige to an unwanted identity; third, the transitional period has created a special class fraction – rural–urban migrant workers – who are neither peasants because they are employed in urban industrial and service sectors, nor urban working class because they mostly have non-urban *hukou* and thus are legally and institutional peasants. Their capacity of being a witness of the transitional Chinese society lies in their position of leaving farming land and thus leaving their peasant identity in response to the increase of labour demand from the urban industry as a result of the economic reform; they work as industrial workers but they are not identified as urban working class because of their peasant identities. Statistics show that among one hunderd occupations and occupation-related identities, 'migrant worker' is ranked ninety-four, and the bottom ten occupation categories are all typically occupied by migrant workers. The statistic result is interpreted that migrant workers are a group of lower class (Li & Tang, 2002), a class fraction lower than urban working class.

The identity making of the migrant workers and migrant children studied in the present research is lodged in this bottom stratum of the urban society. The discursive process of identity construction is the focal point of this book, and language is undoubtedly central in recent identity studies (De Fina *et al.*, 2006). The identity making is, however, more than a linguistic process. Further, it is my conviction that sociolinguistics is better served by engaging in conversation with, and by being able to contribute to wider social scientific discussions. In the present study, the way people dress, the way they move, the house they live in, their jobs, their leisure time activities and their taste (cf. Bourdieu, 1984), all function alongside language use in expressing, performing, negotiating and categorising migrant identities. Underneath these identity expressions and negotiations, we can distinguish an embodied social structure in the individual, or what Bourdieu calls 'habitus', an internalised scheme that has been formed in the course of collective and individual histories, that is inscribed in the body of the individual, and that is expressed through social practice (Bourdieu, 1984: 467). Discursive practice is a crucial product of habitus, but it always interacts with non-discursive practices. Several examples of the analytical chapters can elaborate this argument. First, in the drawing class example (Example 4.1), a migrant pupil draws me with an imagined rural hairstyle, a perhaps familiar hairstyle to her, judged from her conversations with another migrant pupil. In the fields of developmental psychology and educational research, there are theories and research around children's drawing of imagined objects (e.g. Cox, 1992, 1993). The immediate relevance to this case is that the imagined hairstyle perceived as 'rural' is an emblem of the migrant pupil's early year experiences as a rural child, and this early individual history has been incorporated, or is in a process of incorporation, into her habitus. Although being very young, the migrant pupil's individual habitus is structured with the collective history of the country – the rural–urban divide as a result of the collective history over the last five decades or so. As such, non-discursive elements such as hairstyle intertwined with the pupils' discursive practice in the negotiation and construction of the migrant identities.

Another telling example is the 'changing clothes on the bus' case (Example 5.2). In the reported row between migrant workers and an urban bus driver, the migrant construction workers are low-paid migrants who dress and behave in line with the stereotypes of low-paid migrants. The stigma they have is a stigma of being migrant workers, but also a stigma of being lower social class. The social structure is embodied in the migrant workers' socialised bodies and expressed through their lifestyle, their clothes and their encounters with others in the urban social space. Although the incident is instantaneous, it points to the migrant workers' individual history of being peasants and migrants, to the collective history of the rural–urban divide, and to the current social class reformation at a macro level. The non-discursive elements observed in this case, as well as in the other examples of this book, are a crucial dimension of identity construction if we position them within in a wider context of social stratification, and through nuanced analysis of these identity making incidents we begin to gain an understanding of the transitional Chinese society at a macro level.

Methodological Reflections

In this section, I reflect on the selection of data and the motivation of their choice, and on the researcher's position. The data selection of this research can be summarised by the 'key incident approach' (Kroon & Sturm, 2007). As introduced in Chapter 2, 'key incidents' are episodes or events that re-occur in the fieldwork and that have sustaining impacts on the researched people, community or society. An incident can be counted as 'key' because it represents concrete events that reflect the work of abstract principles of social organisation and social norms of practice. The selection of 'key incidents' involves pulling out recurrent events and events which have sustaining influence from the data pool, relating it to other incidents, events, phenomena and theories.

In what follows, I will zoom in on one example (Example 4.4) and reflect on the use of the key incident approach in the data selection. In this metapragmatic discourse of a teacher on a migrant pupil's language and identities, Miss Zhang pointed out that the language 'problem' of Hong, a migrant pupil, was that she did not distinguish [n] and [l] in pronunciation. During the course of the interview, another teacher joined the conversation and gave her example of making 'mistakes' due to this linguistic feature when she travelled to Sichuan. This type of metapragmatic discourses on migrant pupils' linguistic features recurred frequently throughout my fieldwork. Similar linguistic features include the lack of distinctions between the dental sibilants *z* [ts], *c* [ts'], *s* [s], and the retroflexes *zh* [chr], *ch* [ch'r], *sh* [shr] in some dialects, and the use of vernacular lexicon such as '*za*' instead of standard '*zenme*' (meaning 'what') and '*an*' instead of '*wo*' (meaning 'I'). Such metapragmatic discourses articulated by teachers were always related to migrant pupils' place of origin and family background, and as shown in Chapter 4, had an impact on the pupils' identity construction as well as on their academic development. Example 4.4 was an instance of the working of the school's institutional principles on normalising the standard language and on inscribing the hegemonic domination of Putonghua into the linguistic habitus of the pupils. This incident was positioned on the metapragmatic scale of the three-scale framework, and it was linked to the incidents of the other two scales through the notion of indexicality. Together with other examples, it pointed to social practice of identity making as a layered discursive process, of which linguistic features, metapragmatic evaluations, and public discourses functioned at different levels, and interacted and intertwined with each other as well.

The second part of this methodological reflection is concerned with the researcher's position in the fieldwork and in the data analysis. The researcher assumed different roles in different stage of the fieldwork and different roles when deploying different research instruments. For non-participant observation, I was an observer sitting in the corner watching the pupils and the teachers, and for participant observation, my role was that of an English teacher. In group and individual interviews, I was a listener and a speaker engaged in a conversation. At the early stage of the fieldwork, I was a stranger to the pupils and the teachers, whereas I became a friend to some of them when spending longer time in the fieldwork sites. Throughout the fieldwork, I had been a document collector who was interested in all textual and visual documents. My role of a document collector continues, as Beijing is a huge fieldwork site and my role of a fieldworker never ends.

As an ethnographer, I was not detached from the researched people and communities. In Example 3.3, I was an interested customer who had a chat with the street vendor on his business, as well as on his language and identities; in Example 4.1, I was involved in the heated debates between the two migrant pupils, while observing their drawing activities; in Example 5.3, I had a conversation with the school staff and problematised their pragmatic attitudes towards the school award system. Since the very beginning of the fieldwork, my role had been a tool of the ethnographic research. In observation, I was the research tool that was watching, listening, making sense of what I saw and heard, and noting down strange or interesting moments. During interviews, I was part of the conversations, an interlocutor who was interested in the migrants' language and life. In these conversation-like interviews, most interviewees were relaxed and free to give as rich information as possible. It is worth noting that, although I did my utmost in limiting my influence on the interviewees, it was inevitable that my role as a researcher, my accent, my identity of being a local, would creep into the interviews and have an impact on the responses of the interviewees. It would be unwise for any researcher, I believe, to pretend that the interviews she conducted were free from her own impacts. What a researcher could do is to minimise such impacts and to reflect on such occasions adequately in data analysis, such as the reflexive remarks in the analysis of Example 4.3 in Chapter 4.

To sum up, the methodological reflections have been centred on two issues: the motivation of the data selection and the researcher's roles. The researcher's position in the present ethnographic study was to act as a tool of data collection. It is thus crucial to be reflexive on the observer's effect she or he brings to the fieldwork sites, and to be reflexive on the impacts she or he has on the interviewees.

This research leads me into the world of migrant workers and their children in Beijing, a community which is present in every corner of our life yet is often invisible, living in the fringe of the city as well as of the society. From their life, their language use and their identity making practices, we start obtaining an insight of the position of migrant workers in the stratified society, and their contesting identities in the remaking of social structure during the transitional period of the economic and social reformation.

Notes

1. Although people were strictly defined by their family backgrounds at birth (*jiating chushen*) in the 'proletarian' era.
2. Source: *http://www.npc.gov.cn/npc/xinwen/rdlt/rdjs/2008-02/27/content_1400091.htm*, the official website of the National People's Congress. Last accessed on 15.7.09.
3. Source: http://www.gov.cn/jrzg/2008-03/13/content_918514.htm. Last accessed on 15.7.09. About the All-China Federation of Trade Unions see: http://english.acftu.org/template/10002/file.jsp?cid = 63&aid = 156. Last accessed on 15.7.09.
4. One of the four centrally administered cities.
5. Source: http://www.taoyuandj.cn/xnc/sannongjingji/200710/11308.htm. Last accessed on 15.7.09.
6. Figure source: personal communication with a human resource agent.
7. Figure source: http://www.gmw.cn/01gmrb/2009-04/09/content_906955.htm. Last accessed on 15.7.09.

Appendix 1
Overview of Data Collection

As the following table will show, this research took me to a variety of fieldwork sites, and it yielded a complex set of diverse data. The main fieldwork period ran from 2006 to 2008, and it yielded (apart from a huge volume of fieldnotes) upwards of 40 hours of audio-recorded material, hundreds of photos and a huge collection of documents including official documents, students' written texts and drawings and so on.

Activity	Fields	Data type	Features
Prior to fieldwork			
Document collections	Libraries, government official websites, academic journals, the Internet	Government policies, official statistics, media reports, library archives, academic research reports	Public sphere discourses on language and identity
During fieldwork			
Serendipitous observations	Migrant neighbourhood, local shops, working places of migrant workers	Audio recordings of conversations Fieldnotes Photos	Micro linguistic shifts of accents (Examples 3.2 and 3.3)
Participant observations	Privately run migrant school	Audio recordings of class sessions Fieldnotes Photos	Migrant pupils' interaction with each other, with their migrant teachers and with the researcher as a local Beijing people
Non-participant observations	Public primary school (Beili School)	Audio recordings of class sessions Fieldnotes Photos	Migrant pupils' interaction with each other and with local Beijing people (Examples 4.1 and 4.2)

Overview of Data Collection

Individual interviews of teachers and pupils	Privately run migrant school Public primary school (Beili School)	Audio recordings of interviews Fieldnotes	Metapragmatic evaluations on language and identity (Examples 4.3, 4.4 and 5.3)
Group interviews of pupils	Privately run migrant school Public primary school (Beili School)	Audio recordings of interviews Fieldnotes	Metapragmatic evaluations on language and identity (Example 4.2)
Document collections	Privately run migrant school Public primary school (Beili school)	School regulations, school notice board, photos of class sessions and school activities, documents of pupils' essays, course books, drawings of classroom displays, teachers' blackboard displays, etc	Institutional discourses on language and identity (Examples 3.1 and 5.1) Individual identity making discourses
Questionnaires	Public primary school (Beili School)	1 Teachers' evaluations on student language use and school performance 2 Migrant parents' attitudes and anticipations of their children's academic career and development	General information of migrant students and of their parents
After fieldwork			
Document collections	Libraries, government official websites, academic journals, the Internet	Blog discussions, news, statistics	Public and institutional discourses on migrant workers (Example 5.2)
Interviews with migrants, ongoing observations of everyday life	Migrant neighbourhood	Audio recordings of interviews Fieldnotes Photos	Stories of everyday migrant life (Example 6.1)

Appendix 2
Chinese Texts and Pinyin Transcripts of Examples

Example 3.1

题目 普通话让我融入这个城市
宁波日报 10月31日

作者：慈溪市附海中心小学 王燕丹

去年夏天，我随父母从家乡四川来到了这个陌生的城市——宁波。这儿的一切让我感到新奇：鳞次栉比的高楼大厦，宽阔平坦的柏油马路，五彩缤纷的霓虹灯。然而，这一切对我来说既遥远又陌生，因为我是一名外地人，一个民工的子女。

爸爸千辛万苦为我联系了一所学校。开学第一天，爸爸陪我来到了新学校。"哇！"学校好大又好美！我的班主任是一位既年轻又漂亮的女教师。她讲一口标准的普通话，字正腔圆，真好听！她让我在同学面前作一番自我介绍。我嗫嚅地说："俺不会说普通话，俺怎么介绍自己来？"张老师亲切地说："就用家乡话把心里想说的告诉大家就行了。"我吞吞吐吐地说："大家好，俺是来自四川的娃子，以后请……"话未说完，大家就哄堂大笑，我的脸"噌"地就红到耳根，站在那里手足无措，要知道在老家的学校我也是个优等生，何曾受到过这样的嘲笑！最后还是张老师帮我解了围："这有什么好笑的？她说的可是标准的四川话哩。

课后，张老师找我谈话："你得学习普通话，否则的话会给你今后的学习、生活带来很大的困难，你明白吗？"

"嗯！"我用力地点点头。

"有新华字典吗？"张老师问。我摇摇头。

张老师顺手拿过桌上一本崭新的字典说："这本字典送给你，学普通话时用得着，有什么不懂你来找我。"

望着张老师美丽的脸庞，我暗暗下定决心：一定要把普通话学好，决不辜负张老师的一片关怀之情。

清晨，当第一缕霞光洒向大地时，我已早早地起床，搬起小凳，坐在门口，大声地朗读着课文。老乡时不时帮我指正，房东阿姨八岁的女儿也成了我的老师。在学校，听老师上课成了我学习普通话最好的机会。我认真地听着老师的每个发音，并在心里默念。课间我经常向同学们请教，同学们看我如此认真也不再取笑我了，一个个争着当起了我的小老师："我是中国人，我在宁波读书。"我一个字一个字地跟着他们读，他们一个字一个字地帮我纠正。

一天，我和爸爸妈妈一起上街。"看，天一广场。"我指着前面的广告牌一字一顿地大声说。我不再害怕带有浓重的四川口音而不敢大声说话了。我终于消除了语言的隔阂，融入了这座城市。

Example 3.3

Pinyin Transcript

{traffic noise, people talk unintelligibly}

1   Xiao Xu: ni yao *shen me [shrən² mə] de (baozi)*? {weak and slow voice, noticeably trying to pronounce in local Beijing accent}
    JD: ni zhe er dou you shen me de ya?
5   Xiao Xu: you ...
                ... {conversations about the kinds of steamed dumplings he offers}
    JD: nimen zhe er de shengyi tinghao de, zheme duo ren dou mai nimen de baozi.
    Xiao Xu: {laughing voice}*jiushi* zaoshang hao, daole xiawu jiu <u>mei</u>
10   <u>ren</u> chi baozi le {still making efforts to speak in Beijing accent}.
    JD: zaoshang shengyi hao jiu xingle. Neige xia de ni fang jin qu le ma?
    Xiao Xu: {nod with smile}nei tinghao de – women cong <u>laojia</u> dailai
15   de.
    JD: zhende?! Shi na er ya?
    Xiao Xu: {proud, smile} women de xia doushi <u>changjiang</u> li de xia ... **tebie haochi** [t'ə⁴ xo³ k'e¹] {noticeably higher and faster, with clearer accent}.
20 ... {conversations about how they brought the shrimps from their hometown}
    JD: ni Putonghua shuo de ting hao de, zai xuexiao li xuede {smile}?
    Xiao Xu: *hai xing ba*. You de (gu ke) ye buzhidao wo shuo shenme
25   {end with laughing voice, indicating this is a humble response}
    JD: wo juede ni de Putonghua zhen tinghao de, wo tingde ting qingchu de ya.

	Xiao Xu:	en, zai xuexiao li xuede. Wo du <u>dao</u> **gao zhong** [kau¹ chrɔŋ¹]
30		ne
		{switches from noticeable southern accent to near-Putonghua}.
		Ni jiu shi [ni³ chyiu̯ ⁴ shrı̯ ⁴] Beijing ren? {smile, and switch to certain characteristics of Beijing accent}
	JD:	ai. Wo jiushi zhe er de.
35	Xiao Xu:	*jiushi zhe er de* [chyiu̯ ⁴ shrı̯ ⁴ chrer̯ ⁴ de] {low voice, Beijing accent}
	JD:	nimen zai xuexiao <u>quan</u> yong Putonghua?
	Xiao Xu:	women xue (Putonghua), ye shuo nei zhong fangyan.
	JD:	na ni zenme lian de ya {smile}?
40	Xiao Xu:	wo ... wo zai zhe er **dai guo** [tai¹ kuɔ] {switch to Beijing accent, higher, long, jolly voice, indicating he was pleased by my comment on his
		Putonghua, and was proud that he was not a stranger to the city of Beijing}
45	JD:	na ni dou ting de dong zhe er ren shuo hua ma?
	Xiao Xu:	ting de dong, jiu shi bie ren **shuo fangyan** [fɒŋ ¹¹ ien²²] wo ting bu dong {switches back to Putonghua}.
	JD:	= nashi. Bie ren shuo fangyan wo ye ting bu dong.
	Xiao Xu:	= youde shuo <u>fangyan</u>, wo bantian buzhidao shenme ne
50		{end with laughing voice, amused}
	JD:	jiu shi; erqie zhe di er ba, na er de ren dou you, suoyi na er de fangyan dou you ...

Chinese Texts and Pinyin Transcripts of Examples

Example 5.1

农民工之家　就业指导

进城务工前
练好普通话

城务工的障碍。但是对南方以及一些边远地区的人来说，如果自己家乡的方言与普通话相差甚远，自己的口音又很重，进城之前练好普通话就极为迫切了。否则，你在城市将寸步难行。大量的事实都证明，普通话是农村富余劳动力进城务工的一道门槛。

普通话是以北京语音为标准音，以北方话为基础方言，以典范的现代白话文著作为语法规范的现代汉民族的共同语。简单的说，就是我们平常在电视上看到的新闻报道，说的就是普通话。现在全国大力推广普通话，绝大多数的城市都以普通话为主要沟通语言。而 1997 年召开的全国语言文字工作会议确定了新世纪我国语言文字的目标，要求在 2010 年以前，普通话在全国范围内初步普及，21 世纪中叶以前在全国范围内普及。

对于北方农村的人来说，普通话一般不会成为进

练好普通话，不仅能使自己在应聘时给对方留下一个好的形象，增加找工作的成功率。同时，又能保证让别人理解自己所说的话，更好的表达自己的想法，让别人认识和了解自己。这样才能在城市立稳脚跟，找到自己适合的工作。如果一个人说的话别人都听不清楚，即使他工作干的很好，但不能跟人有效的沟通，就会给人一种无法信任的感觉，这无形之中就削弱了自己的竞争力。同时，语言上的障碍也会使自己不能与其他人交流思想、感情，这使自己显得很孤立，在情感的满足上存在着遗憾。所以，重视普通话训练是必要的。

Example 5.2
The online news report on the 'changing clothes incident'

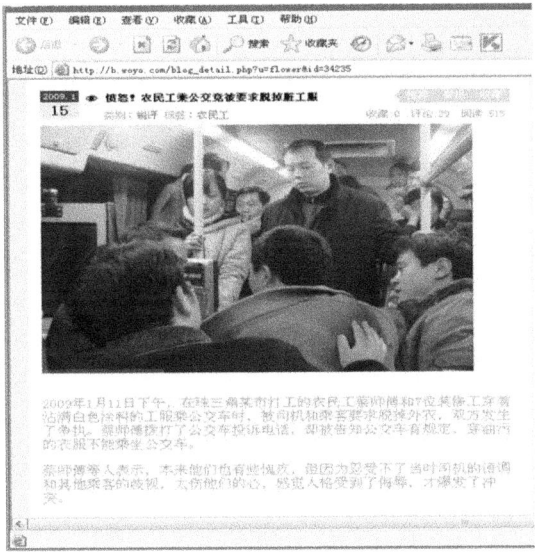

The debate entries of online forums

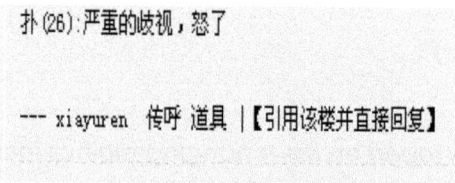

Responses 4, 5, 6, 7, 8 and 9.

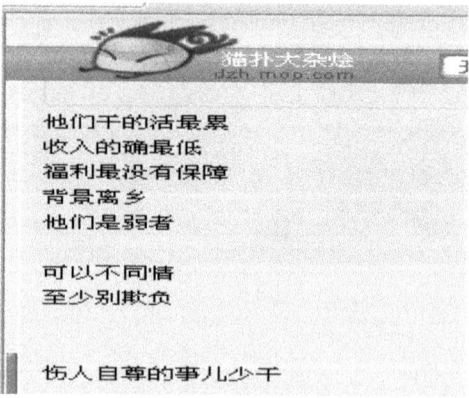

Response 26.

Responses sympathetic to the migrant workers.

猫(67):就不能好好说吗,态度！！

民工也是,可以自觉一点就行。

猫(147):虽然是有上车的权利,但是也要遵守公共秩序,及公共卫生。这也应尽的义务。没有遵守业务哪来的权利

--- gan6610   传呼 道具 |【引用该楼并直接回复】

Responses 67 and 147 that blame both sides.

--- 天行健www   传呼 道具 |【引用该楼并直接回复】

猫(149):我可不认为是岐视,在雨天我们坐公交车的时候还要收雨具脱雨衣呢,一个意思!!!

扑(20):公众场所,要照顾到他人,约束自己的行为,如同在公众场所禁止吸烟一样,如果你感冒了,请到室外去解决,这难道也是一种岐视?！只能说现在大部分人公德意识淡薄,动不动还扯上岐视。这些民工上车前自己就应该意识到这一点,没有意识,非要让别人说出来,说脸的就只有自己。

--- zhjy5638 传呼 道具 |【引用该楼并直接回复】

Responses 149 and 20 that are on the bus driver's side.

猫(21):这个事例很典型
再说几句
现在有些人总认为自己是弱者
会受到别人不公正的待遇
别人如果说一些正当要求
就认为自己受到岐视————这样不好
首先不要有自卑感
端正好自己的心态
相互尊重
社会公德任何人都必须尊守

Response 21 that blames the migrant workers.

References

Agha, A. (2007) *Language and Social Relations*. Cambridge: Cambridge University Press.
Anderson, P. (1998) *The Origins of Postmodernity*. London: Verso.
Antaki, C. and Widdicombe, S. (eds) (1998) *Identity in Talk*. London: Sage.
Barley, N. (1987) *A Plague of Caterpillars: A Return to the African Bush*. New York: Penguin.
Bauman, Z. (1991) *Modernity and Ambivalence*. Cambridge: Polity Press.
Bezemer, J. (2003) *Dealing with Multilingualism in Education. A Case Study of a Dutch Primary School Classroom*. Amsterdam: Aksant Academic Publishers.
Bezemer, J. and Kroon, S. (2006) 'You don't need to know the Turkish word': Immigrant minority language teaching policies and practice in the Netherlands. *Educational Studies in Language and Literature* 6, 13–29.
Blackledge, A. (2005) *Discourse and Power in a Multilingual World*. Amsterdam: John Benjamins.
Block, D. (2006) *Multilingual Identities in a Global City: London Stories*. London: Palgrave.
Blommaert, J. (1999) *State Ideology and Language in Tanzania*. Cologne: Rudiger Köppe Verlag.
Blommaert, J. (2001) Context is/as critique. *Critique of Anthropology* 21, 13–32.
Blommaert, J. (2004) *Workshopping: Professional Vision, Practices and Critique in Discourse Analysis*. Ghent: Academia.
Blommaert, J. (2005a) *Discourse: A Critical Introduction*. Cambridge: Cambridge University Press.
Blommaert, J. (2005b) In and out of class, codes and control. In M. Baynham and A. De Fina (eds) *Dislocations/Relocations: Narratives of Displacement* (pp. 127–143). Manchester: St Jerome.
Blommaert, J. (2006a) Sociolinguistic scales. *Working Papers in Urban Language and Literacies* 37, 1–15.
Blommaert, J. (2006b) Language ideology. In K. Brown (ed.) *Encyclopedia of Language and Linguistics* (2nd edn, Vol. 6, pp. 510–522). Oxford: Elsevier.
Blommaert, J. (2009a) A market of accent. *Language Policy* 8, 243–259.
Blommaert, J. (2009b) Language, asylum, and the national order. *Current Anthropology* 50, 415–441.
Blommaert, J. (2009c) *The Sociolinguistics of Globalisation*. Cambridge: Cambridge University Press.
Blommaert, J., Collins, J. and Slembrouck, S. (2005a) Spaces of multilingualism. *Language and Communication* 25, 197–216.
Blommaert, J., Collins, J. and Slembrouck, S. (2005b) Polycentricity and interactional regimes in 'global neighborhoods'. *Ethnography* 6, 205–235.

Blommaert, J., Creve, L. and Willaert, E. (2006) On being declared illiterate: Language-ideological disqualification in Dutch classes for immigrants in Belgium. *Language and Communication* 26, 34–54.
Blommaert, J. and Dong, J. (2009) Language and movement in space. In N. Coupland (ed.) *Handbook of Language and Globalisation*. Oxford: Blackwell.
Blommaert, J. and Dong, J. (2010) *Ethnographic Fieldwork: A Beginner's Guide*. Bristol: Multilingual Matters.
Blommaert, J. and Verschueren, J. (1998) *Debating Diversity*. London: Routledge.
Bloomfield, L. (1927) Literate and illiterate speech. *American Speech* 2, 432–439.
Bourdieu, P. (1984) *Distinction: A Social Critique of the Judgement of Taste*. Cambridge, MA: Harvard University Press.
Bourdieu, P. (1987) In other words. In J. Revel and L. Hunt (eds) (1995), *Histories. French Constructions of the Past* (pp. 514–520). New York: The New Press.
Bourdieu, P. (1990) *The Logic of Practice*. Cambridge: Polity Press.
Bourdieu, P. (1991) *Language and Symbolic Power*. Cambridge: Polity Press.
Briggs, C. (1997) Introduction: From the ideal, the ordinary, and the orderly to conflict and violence in pragmatic research. *Pragmatics* 7, 451–459.
Bucholtz, M., Liang, A.C. and Sutton, L.A. (1999) *Reinventing Identities*. Oxford: Oxford University Press.
Butler, J. (1990) *Gender Trouble: Feminism and the Subversion of Identity*. New York: Routledge.
Butler, T. and Robson, G. (2003) *London Calling: The Middle Classes and the Re-Making of Inner London*. Oxford: Berg.
Cameron, D. (1992) *Feminism and Linguistic Theory*. London: Macmillan.
Chen, P. (1999) *Modern Chinese: History and Sociolinguistics*. Cambridge: Cambridge University Press.
China Daily (2004) Greater numbers speak Mandarin. On WWW at http://www.chinadaily.com.cn/english/doc/204-12/26/content_403419.htm. Accessed 15.7.06.
Chouliaraki, L. and Fairclough, N. (1999) *Discourse in Late Modernity: Rethinking Critical Discourse Analysis*. Edinburgh: Edinburgh University Press.
Coblin, W.S. (2000) A brief history of Mandarin. *Journal of the American Oriental Society* 120, 537–552.
Coupland, N. (2007) *Style: Language Variation and Identity*. Cambridge: Cambridge University Press.
Cox, M. (1992) *Children's Drawing*. Harmondsworth: Penguin Book.
Cox, M. (1993) *Children's Drawing of the Humane Figure*. Hillsdale, NJ: Erlbaum.
De Fina, A., Schiffrin, D. and Bamberg, M. (2006) Introduction. In A. De Fina (ed.) *Discourse and Identity* (pp. 1–23). Cambridge: Cambridge University Press.
De Francis, J. (1984) *The Chinese Language: Fact and Fantasy*. Honolulu: University of Hawaii Press.
De Saussure, F. (1972) *Course in General Linguistics*. (R. Harries, trans.). Chicago: Open Court.
D'hondt, S. (2001) Conversation analysis and history: Practical and discursive understandings of quarrels among Dar es Salaam adolescents. PhD thesis, University of Antwerp.

Dong, J. (2009) 'Isn't it enough to be a Chinese speaker': Language ideology and migrant identity construction in a public primary school in Beijing. *Language and Communication* 29, 115–126.
Dong, J. (2010a) The enregisterment of Putonghua in practice. *Language and Communication* 30, 265–275.
Dong, J. (2010b) Neo-liberalism and the evolvement of China's education policies on migrant children's schooling. *The Journal for Critical Education Policy Studies* 8, 137–160.
Dong, J. and Blommaert, J. (2009) Space, scale and accents: Constructing migrant identity in Beijing. *Multilingua* 28, 1–24.
Erickson, F. (1977) Some approaches to inquiry in school–community ethnography. *Anthropology and Education Quarterly* 8, 58–69.
Extra, G., Spotti, M. and Van Avermaet, P. (2009) *Language Testing, Migration and Citizenship*. London: Continuum.
Fabian, J. (1995) Ethnographic misunderstanding and the perils of context. *American Anthropologist* 97, 41–50.
Fairclough, N. (1992) *Discourse and Social Change*. Cambridge: Polity Press.
Fairclough, N. (1996) A reply to Henry Widdowson's 'Discourse analysis: A critical view'. *Language and Literature* 5, 49–56.
Fan, X.Z. (2004) Liudong ertong jiaoyu mianlin de zhengce wenti yu duice. *Jiaoyu yu Jingji* 4, 1–5. [On the financial problems facing the education of the floating children and some countermeasures. *Education and Economics* 4, 1–5.]
Fan, X.Z. (2005) Liudong ertong jiaoyu mianlin de wenti yu duice. *Dangdai Jiaoyu Luntan* 2, 24–29. [Migrant children's educational difficulties and possible solutions. *Contemporary Education Forum* 2, 24–29.]
Foucault, M. (1984) *The History of Sexuality*. Harmondsworth: Penguin.
Foucault, M. (2003) *Abnormal*. New York: Picador.
Gao, Y. (2009) Language and identity: State of the art and a debate of legitimacy. In J. Lo Bianco, J. Orton and Y. Gao (eds) *China and English: Globalization and Dilemmas of Identity*. Bristol: Multicultural Matters.
Gao, Y. and Xiu, L. (2004) 'We could be heros, just for one day': Investment in English songs and movies and construction of multiple identities. *Teaching English in China* 2008, 93–101.
Gao, Y., Xiu, L. and Kuang, W. (2007a) 'I want to be a captain of my own heart': English names and EFL learners' multiple identity construction. In Shi-xu (ed.) *Unpublished Proceedings of the Second International Conference on Multicultural Discourses*.
Gao, Y., Zhao, Y., Cheng, Y. and Zhou, Y. (2007b) Relationships between English learning motivation types and self-identity changes among Chinese students. *TESOL Quarterly* 41, 133–155.
Georgakopoulou, A. (2006) Small and large identities in narrative (inter)action. In A. De Fina, D. Schiffrin and M. Bamberg (eds) *Discourse and Identity* (pp. 83–102). Cambridge: Cambridge University Press.
Giddens, A. (1990) *The Consequences of Modernity*. Cambridge: Polity Press.
Giddens, A. (1991) *Modernity and Self-Identity. Self and Society in the Late Modern Age*. Cambridge: Polity Press.
Goffman, E. (1974a) *Frame Analysis: An Essay on the Organization of Experience*. New York: Harper & Row.

Goffman, E. (1974b) *Stigma: Notes on the Management of Spoiled Identity*. New York: Jason Aronson.
Goffman, E. (1981) *Forms of Talk*. Philadelphia: University of Pennsylvania Press.
Gogolin, I. (1998) The 'monolingual habitus' as a tertium comparison in the international comparison of teaching in the language of the majority. In G. Khruslov and S. Kroon (eds) *The Challenge of Multilingualism to Standard Language Teaching. Cases from Flanders, England, The Netherlands, Germany and Russia* (pp. 157–166). Moscow: INPO.
Green, J. and Bloome, D. (1997) Ethnography and ethnographers in education: A situated perspective. In J. Flood, S.B. Heath and D. Lapp (eds) *Handbook of Research on Teaching Literacy through the Communicative and Visual Arts* (pp. 181–202). New York: Macmillan.
Gumperz, J. (1968) *The Speech Community. International Encyclopaedia of the Social Sciences* (pp. 381–386). London: Macmillan.
Gumperz, J. (2003) Response essay. In S. Eerdmans, C. Prevignano and P. Thibault (eds) *Language and Interaction Discussions with John J. Gumperz* (pp. 105–123). Amsterdam: John Benjamins Publishing.
Gumperz, J. and Hymes, D. (eds) (1972) *Direction in Sociolinguistics: The Ethnography of Communication*. London: Blackwell.
Guo, F. and Gao, S.B. (2003) Yayan, tongyu, guanhua, Putonghua: Han minzu tongyongyu yange jianshuo. *Guyuan Shizhuan Xuebao* 5, 70–72. [Yayan, tongyu, guanhua, Putonghua: A brief account of the development of Han Chinese common language. *Journal of Guyuan Teachers College* 5, 70–72.]
Han, J. (2001) Beijing shi liudong ertong yiwu jiaoyu zhuangkuang diaocha baogao. *Qingnian Yanjiu* 8, 1–18. [Survey report on the state of compulsory education among migrant children in Beijing. *Youth Research* 8, 1–18.]
Harvey, D. (1990) *The Condition of Postmodernity: An Enquiry into the Origins of Cultural Change*. Cambridge, MA: Blackwell.
Harvey, D. (2001) *Spaces of Capital: Towards a Critical Geography*. Edinburgh: Edinburgh University Press.
Hewitt, R. (1986) *White Talk Black Talk: Inter-Racial Friendship and Communication among Adolescents*. Cambridge: Cambridge University Press.
Hinnenkamp, V. (1991) Talking a person into interethnic distinction: A discourse-analytic case study. In J. Blommaert and J. Verschueren (eds) *The Pragmatics of Intercultural and International Communication* (pp. 151–175). Amsterdam: John Benjamins.
Hobsbawm, E. and Ranger, T. (eds) (1983) *The Invention of Tradition*. Cambridge: Cambridge University Press.
Hu, M.Y. (1987) *Beijinghua Chutan*. Beijing: Shangwu Yinshu Guan. [*An Exploration of Beijing Dialect*. Beijing: Commercial Press.]
Hu, Y.S. (1995) *Xiandai Hanyu*. Shanghai: Shanghai Jiaoyu Chubanshe. [*Modern Chinese*. Shanghai: Shanghai Education Press.]
Hymes, D. (1964) *Language in Culture and Society. A Reader in Linguistics and Anthropology*. New York: Harper & Row.
Hymes, D. (1968) Linguistic problems in defining the concept of 'tribe'. In J. Helm (ed.) *Essays on the Problem of Tribe* (pp. 23–48). Seattle: American Ethnological Society and University of Washington Press.
Hymes, D. (1980) *Language in Education: Ethnolinguistic Essays*. Washington, DC: Centre for Applied Linguistics.

Hymes, D. (1981) *In Vain I Tried to Tell You: Essays in Native American Ethnopoetics*. Philadelphia: University of Pennsylvania Press.
Hymes, D. (1996) *Ethnography, Linguistics, Narrative Inequality: Towards an Understanding of Voice*. London: Taylor & Francis.
Irvine, J. and Gal, S. (2000) Language ideology and linguistic differentiation. In P. Kroskrity (ed.) *Regimes of Language: Ideologies, Polities, and Identities* (pp. 35–83). Santa Fe: School of American Research Press.
Johnstone, B., Andrus, J. and Danielson, A. (2006) Mobility, indexicality, and the enregisterment of 'Pittsburghese'. *Journal of English Linguistics* 34, 77–104.
Knight, J. and Song, L. (1999) *The Rural–Urban Divide: Economic Disparities and Interactions in China*. Oxford: Oxford University Press.
Kratochvil, P. (1968) *The Chinese Language Today*. London: Hutchinson University Library.
Kress, G. and van Leeuwen, T. (1996) *Reading Images: The Grammar of Visual Design*. London: Routledge.
Kroon, S. (1986) Interkultureller Sprachunterricht. *Diskussion Deutsch* 17, 413–423.
Kroon, S. and Sturm, J. (2007) International comparative case study research in education: Key incident analysis and international triangulation. In W. Herrlitz, S. Ongstad and P.H. van de Ven (eds) *Research on Mother Tongue Education in a Comparative International Perspective. Theoretical and Methodological Issues* (pp. 99–118). Amsterdam: Rodopi.
Kroon, S. and Vallen, T. (1991) Monolinguale Lehrer in multilingualen Klassen. In I. Gogolin, S. Kroon, M. Krüger-Potratz, U. Neumann and T. Vallen (Hrsg.), *Kultur- und Sprachenvielfalt in Europa* (pp. 125–149). Münster: Waxmann.
Kroskrity, P. (ed.) (2000) *Regimes of Language: Ideologies, Polities, and Identities*. Santa Fe: SAR Press.
Kuijs, L. and Wang, T. (2005) China's pattern of growth: Moving to sustainability and reducing inequality. *World Bank China Office Research Working Paper*, 2. Beijing: World Bank.
Kulick, D. (1998) *Travesti: Sex, Gender and Culture among Brazilian Transgendered Prostitutes*. Chicago: University of Chicago Press.
Lefebvre, H. (2003) Levels and dimensions. In S. Elden, E. Lebas and E. Kofman (eds) *Henri Lefebvre: Key Writings*. New York: Continuum.
Lei, H. (2009) Language learning and language use of pre-school children in Shanghai. Paper, *7th International Symposium on Bilingualism*, Utrecht, July 2009.
Li, Q. and Tang, Z. (2002) Chengshi nongmingong yu chengshi zhong de fei zhenggui jiuye. *Shehuixue Yanjiu* 6. [Migrant workers in cities and urban informal employment. *Sociology Research* 6.]
Li, W. (1998) The 'why' and 'how'm questions in the analysis of conversational code-switching. In P. Auer (ed.) *Code-switching in Conversation: Language, Interaction, and Identity*. London: Routledge.
Li, W. (2004) Conflicting notions of language purity: The interplay of archaising, ethnographic, reformist, elitist and xenophobic purism in the perception of Standard Chinese. *Language & Communication* 24, 97–133.
Lu, S.Q. and Zhang, S.L. (2001) Chengxiang chabie xiade liudong ertong jiaoyu – guanyu Beijing dagong zidi xuexiao de diaocha. *Zhanlue yu Guanli* 4, 95–108. [Urban–rural disparity and migrant children's education. *Strategy and Management* 4, 95–108.]

Lu, X.H. (2005) Lun woguo gujin huji zhidu shehui zhineng jiqi zuoyong de yitong. *Zhongzhou Xuekan* 6. [The similarities and differences of the household registration practices in China's history, social functions and effects. *Academic Journal of Zhongzhou* 6, 256–268.]

Ma, X. (1999) New trends in population migration in China. In T. Scharping (ed.) *Floating Population and Migration in China: The Impact of Economic Reforms* (pp. 56–71). Hamburg: Institut für Asienkunde.

Maryns, K. (2006) *The Asylum Speaker: Language in the Belgian Asylum Procedure*. Manchester: St Jerome.

Massey, D. (1994) *Space, Place and Gender*. Minneapolis: University of Minnesota Press.

Ningbo Daily (2006) Putonghua rang wo rong ru zhege chengshi [Putonghua helps me integrate with this city.] On WWW at http://www.cnnb.com.cn/gb/node2/newspaper/nbrb/2006/10/node69731/node69737/userobject7ai1326148.html. Accessed 15.7.09.

Nongmin Keji Peixun (2005) Jincheng wugong qian lianhao Putonghua. [Practising Putonghua well before entering the city and searching for jobs. Science and Technology Training for Farmers, 1.] On WWW at http://www.cqvip.com/qk/86404X/200501/index.shtml. Accessed 15.7.09.

Norman, J. (1988) *Chinese*. Cambridge: Cambridge University Press.

Norton-Pierce, B. (2000) *Identity and Language Learning: Gender, Ethnicity and Educational Change*. London: Longman.

Ochs, E. (1979) Transcription as theory. In E. Ochs and B. Schieffelin (eds) *Developmental Pragmatics* (pp. 43–72). New York: Academic Press.

Oria, A., Cardini, A., Stamou, E., Kolookitha, M., Vertigan, S., Ball, S. and Flores-Moreno, C. (2007) Urban education, the middle classes and their dilemmas of school choice. *Journal of Education Policy* 22, 91–106.

Potter, J. (2003) Discursive psychology: Between method and paradigm. *Discourse and Society* 14, 783–794.

Potter, J. and Wetherell, M. (1987) *Discourse and Social Psychology: Beyond Attitudes and Behaviour*. London: Sage.

Rampton, B. (1995) *Crossing: Language and Ethnicity among Adolescents*. London: Longman.

Rampton, B. (1998) Speech community. In J. Verschueren, J.-O. Ostman, J. Blommaert and C. Bulcaen (eds) *Handbook of Pragmatics* (pp. 1–30). Amsterdam: John Benjamins.

Rampton, B. (1999) Styling the other. *Journal of Sociolinguistics – Special Issue* 3, 421–427.

Rampton, B. (2005) *Crossing: Language and Ethnicity among Adolescents*. Manchester: St Jerome.

Rampton, B. (2006) *Language in Late Modernity: Interaction in an Urban School*. Cambridge: Cambridge University Press.

Rampton, B. (2008) Speech community and beyond. In N. Coupland and A. Jaworski (eds) *The New Sociolinguistics Reader*. Palgrave Macmillan: Hampshire.

Ramsey, R. (1987) *The Languages of China*. Princeton, NJ: Princeton University Press.

Raveaud, M. and van Zanten, A. (2007) Choosing the local school: Middle class parents' values and social and ethnic mix in London and Paris. *Journal of Education Policy* 22, 107–124.

Reay, D. (2004a) 'It's all becoming a habitus': Beyond the habitual use of habitus in educational research. *British Journal of Sociology of Education* 25, 431–444.
Reay, D. (2004b) 'Mostly Roughs and Toughs': Social class, race and representation in inner city schooling. *Sociology* 35, 1005–1023.
Roosens, E. (1989) *Creating Ethnicity: The Process f Ethnogenesis*. Newbury Park: Sage.
Schegloff, E. (1997) Whose text? Whose context? *Discourse and Society* 8, 165–187.
Schegloff, E. (1999) Talk in social structure. In A. Jaworski and N. Coupland (eds) *The Discourse Reader* (pp. 107–120). London: Routledge.
Schieffelin, B., Woolard, K. and Kroskrity, P. (eds) (1998) *Language Ideologies: Practice and Theory*. New York: Oxford University Press.
Scollon, R. and Scollon, S.W. (2003) *Discourse in Place: Language in the Material World*. London: Routledge.
Silverstein, M. (1979) Language structure and linguistic ideology. In P.R. Clyne, W.F. Hanks and C.L. Hofbauer (eds) *The Elements: A Parasession on Linguistic Units and Levels*. Chicago: Chicago Linguistic Society.
Silverstein, M. (1981) The limits of awareness. *Working Papers in Sociolinguistics* 84. Austin, TX: Southwest Educational Development Library.
Silverstein, M. (1996) Monoglot standard in America: Standardization and metaphors of linguistic hegemony. In D. Brenneis and R. Macaulay (eds) *The Matrix of Language* (pp. 284–306). Boulder: Westview.
Silverstein, M. (1998) Contemporary transformations of local linguistic communities. *Annual Review of Anthropology* 27, 193–229.
Silverstein, M. (2003) Indexical order and the dialectics of sociolinguistic life. *Language and Communication* 23, 193–229.
Silverstein, M. (2004) Cultural concepts and the language–culture nexus. *Current Anthropology* 45, 175–214.
Spotti, M. (2007) *Developing Identities: Identity Construction in Multicultural Primary Classrooms in the Netherlands and Flanders*. Amsterdam: Aksant.
Swyngedouw, E. (1996) Reconstructing citizenship, the re-scaling of the State and the new authoritarianism: Closing the Belgian mines. *Urban Studies* 33, 1499–1521.
Tsou, B. (2009) Transitional triglossia and language shift: Accelerated urbanization in China and language planning. Paper, *7th International Symposium on Bilingualism*, Utrecht, July 2009.
Uitermark, J. (2002) Re-scaling, 'scale fragmentation' and the regulation of antagonistic relationships. *Progress in Human Geography* 26, 743–765.
UNDP (2003) *Millennium Development Goals China's Progress*. Beijing: United Nations Development Programme.
UNDP (2005) *Human Development Report on China*. Beijing: United Nations Development Programme.
Van den Berg, M. (2009) Developing bilingualism in southern China language behaviour in Guangzhou and Shenzhen. Paper, *7th International Symposium on Bilingualism*, Utrecht, July 2009.
Vertovec, S. (2006) The emergence of super-diversity in Britain. *Working Paper*, 25, WP-06-25. Centre on Migration, Policy and Society, University of Oxford.
Wallerstein, I. (1983) *Historical Capitalism*. London: Verso.
Wallerstein, I. (1988) The inventions of TimeSpace realities: Towards an understanding of our historical systems. *Geography* LXXIII, 289–297.

Wallerstein, I. (1991) *Unthinking Social Science: The Limits of Nineteenth-Century Paradigms*. Cambridge: Polity Press.
Wallerstein, I. (1998) The time of space and the space of time: The future of social science. *Political Geography* XVII, 71–82.
Wallerstein, I. (2000) *The Essential Wallerstein*. New York: The New Press.
Wallerstein, I. (2001) *Unthinking Social Science* (2nd edn). Philadelphia: Temple University Press.
Widdowson, H. (1995) Discourse analysis: A critical view. *Language and Literature* 4, 157–172.
Widdowson, H. (1996) Reply to Fairclough: Discourse and interpretation: Conjectures and refutations. *Language and Literature* 5, 57–69.
Widdowson, H. (1998) The theory and practice of Critical Discourse Analysis. *Applied Linguistics* 19, 136–151.
Wilcox, K. (1980) *The Ethnography of Schooling Implications for Educational Policy Making*. Stanford, CA: IREFG.
Willis, P. (1981) *Learning to Labor: How Working Class Kids Get Working Class Jobs*. New York: Columbia University Press.
Wodak, R. (1995) Critical linguistics and critical discourse analysis. In J. Verschueren, J.-O. Ostman, J. Blommaert and C. Bulcaen (eds) *Handbook of Pragmatics: Manual* (pp. 204–210). Amsterdam: John Benjamins.
Wodak, R. (1997) Critical discourse analysis and the study of doctor–patient interaction. In B.L. Gunnarsson, P. Linell and B. Nordberg (eds) *The Construction of Professional Discourse* (pp. 173–200). London: Longman.
Woronov, T.E. (2004) In the eye of the chicken: Hierarchy and marginality among Beijing's migrant schoolchildren. *Ethnography* 5, 289–313.
Wortham, S. (2006) *Learning Identity: The Joint Emergence of Social Identification and Academic Learning*. Cambridge: Cambridge University Press.
Xu, D. (2009) The leveling of tones in the Kundulun speech community. Paper, *7th International Symposium on Bilingualism*, Utrecht, July 2009.
Yu, W. (2009) Language contact effects on language identity: A case study of the high school students in Changzhou city. Paper, *7th International Symposium on Bilingualism*, Utrecht, July 2009.
Zhang, Q.L., Qu, Z.Y. and Zou, H. (2003) Liudong ertong fazhan zhuangkuang diaocha. *Qingnian Yanjiu* 9, 11–17. [An investigation of the development of migrant children in four cities. *Youth Research* 9, 11–17.]
Zhang, W. (2002) *Drifting and Competition: The Changes of The Phonological Structure of Guanzhong Dialects*. Xi'an: Shanxi People's Press.
Zhou, Q. (2003a) Unity in diversity and diversity in unity: Language policy and language planning in China. In Q. Zhou (ed.) *Nation, Ethnicity and Language: Language Policy Studies of Individual Countries*. Beijing: Yuwen Press.
Zhou, Q. (ed.) (2003b) *Nation, Ethnicity and Language: Language Policy Studies of Individual Countries*. Beijing: Yuwen Press.
Zhou, Q. (2005) *The Green Paper of Language Situation in China: 2005*. Beijing: The Commercial Press.
Zhou, Q. (2006) *The Green Paper of Language Situation in China: 2006*. Beijing: The Commercial Press.
Zhou, Q. (2007) *The Green Paper of Language Situation in China: 2007*. Beijing: The Commercial Press.

Zhou, Q. (2008) *The Green Paper of Language Situation in China: 2008*. Beijing: The Commercial Press.
Zhou, Q. (2009) *The Green Paper of Language Situation in China: 2009*. Beijing: The Commercial Press.
Zhu, H. (2008) Duelling languages, duelling values: Codeswitching in bilingual intergenerational conflict talk in diasporic families. *Journal of Pragmatics* 40, 1799–1816.
Zimmerman, D.H. (1998) Identity, context and interaction. In C. Antaki and S. Widdicombe (eds) *Identity in Talk*. London: Sage.
Zou, H., Qu, Z.Y. and Zhang, Q.L. (2005) Zhongguo jiu chengshi liudong ertong fazhan yu xuqiu diaocha. *Qingnian Yanjiu* 2, 1–7. [A survey on the development and needs of migrant children in nine cities in China. *Youth Research* 2, 1–7.]

Index

abnormality 20, 51, 55, 88-91, 94, 99, 100, 102, 104, 110, 111, 115, 116, 121, 132
accent-less 35, 51, 82
anthropology, linguistic 36, 18, 65, 69, 124

Baihuawen 31
Bourdieu, Pierre 52, 56, 73, 126, 133, 134

centre-periphery analysis 27, 49, 50, 54, 55, 59, 61, 63, 64
Conversational Analysis (CA) 5-7
Critical Discourse Analysis (CDA) 8-9

data history 37-41
down-scaling 55, 131-133

educational inequality 16, 36, 48, 58, 104, 109, 110, 122, 124, 128, 129
enregisterment 31
epistemology 18, 36-37
ethnographic fieldwork 18-19
ethnolinguistic identity 69, 70, 73, 85, 122

fangyan 17
footing 65
Foucault, Michael 51, 88-91

globalisation 16, 27, 28, 56, 128
Goffman, Erving 5, 48, 62, 65, 71, 89, 90, 103

habitus 52, 66, 134
– monolingual 53, 55, 56, 66
Han Chinese 17, 29
homogeneity 11, 53, 71, 75, 127, 128
household registration 10, 25
hukou 10, 14, 16, 26, 33, 71, 87, 110, 108, 123
Hymes, Dell 18, 19, 69, 70, 73

identity
– achieved 5, 13, 62, 114
– ascribed 5, 13, 62, 114
– constructed 5
indexicality 11, 48, 78, 85, 118, 123, 124
– order of 55

interview 41, 136, 139
– group 20, 139
– individual 139

key incident approach 42, 135

language ideology 13, 69, 70, 76, 82, 123-126
– monoglot 20, 29, 65, 84, 85, 115, 127
language-less 52, 80
learning process 37-39, 41, 79
Lefebvre, Henri 46
lower class 64, 133

Mandarin 17, 29, 30, 31, 55, 120
metapragmatic 13, 66, 68, 71, 76, 85, 118, 119, 122, 125, 126, 135
migrant worker 7, 20, 58, 59, 66, 89, 94, 95, 111, 116, 132, 133
misrecognition 52, 56
modernism 90
modernity 88, 90

nation-state 51, 90
normality 20, 53, 90, 91, 94, 110, 121

observation 15, 40, 41, 77, 118, 129, 138 136
observer's effect 40
ontology 18, 36, 37
othering 5, 13, 63, 64

petit bourgeoisie 133
post modern 90
Putonghua 29, 32, 56, 64, 75, 94, 119, 131

re-scaling 46
reflexivity/reflexive 41, 79, 94, 136
rural-urban migration 3, 16, 50, 115, 122, 128, 129, 130

scale 11-15, 45-48, 114
– institutional and public 14, 87-111, 120, 122
– linguistic and communicative 12, 45-66, 118, 120

– metapragmatic 13, 68-84, 118, 122
– sociolinguistic 115
social class reformation 134
social fraction 35 128 133
social order 47, 49, 100, 103, 104, 111, 121, 124, 132
social stratification 4, 134
space 4, 7, 19, 20, 26, 34, 45-50, 52, 55, 57-65, 73, 75, 79, 85-88, 92, 95-119, 128
spatiotemporal analysis 11, 15, 45, 49, 117
speech community 20, 51, 68, 69, 70, 85, 115, 123, 149
stereotype 1, 10, 48, 116, 134
stigma 3, 20, 30, 35, 48, 50-56, 72-78, 88-99, 103-116, 134, 149

super-diversity 17 24 152
synchronic deployment 117
synchronised social reality 118

the Communist Revolution 31
the Internet 20, 95- 99, 103-104, 111, 116, 121

up-scaling 63
urbanisation 25

voice 26, 94, 99

Wallerstein 49
World-System Analysis 11, 49

For Product Safety Concerns and Information please contact our EU Authorised Representative:

Easy Access System Europe

Mustamäe tee 50

10621 Tallinn

Estonia

gpsr.requests@easproject.com